KW-326-381

COLLECTION LATOMUS
VOLUME 172

PERVIGILIUM VENERIS

LATOMUS

REVUE D'ÉTUDES LATINES

60, rue Colonel Chaltin, B. 1180 Bruxelles

La revue **Latomus**, fondée en 1937 par M.-A. **Kugener**, L. **Herrmann** et M. **Renard** et dirigée actuellement par MM. Léon Herrmann, Marcel Renard et Guy Cambier, publie des articles, des variétés et discussions, des notes de lecture, des comptes rendus, des notices bibliographiques, des informations pédagogiques ayant trait à tous les domaines de la latinité : textes, littérature, histoire, institutions, archéologie, épigraphie, paléographie, humanisme, etc.

Les quelque **1000 pages** qu'elle comporte actuellement contiennent une riche documentation, souvent **inédite** et abondamment **illustrée**.

Montant de l'abonnement au tome XXXIX (1980) :

Abonnement ordinaire : 1250 FB.

Port et expédition en sus.
Prix des tomes publiés avant l'année en cours : 1500 FB.
Les quatre fascicules d'un tome ne sont pas vendus séparément.

C.C.P. **000-0752646-23** de la **Société d'études latines de Bruxelles.**

Pour l'achat des tomes I à XXI, s'adresser à :
Johnson Reprint Corporation,
111, Fifth Avenue, New York 3, New York.

Correspondants :

ARGENTINE : M. le Prof. Fr. Nóvoa, Laprida, 1718, Buenos-Aires.

BRÉSIL : M. le Prof. Vandick Londres da Nóbrega, 32, Rua Araucaria, Jardim Botanico, Rio-de-Janeiro.

ÉTATS-UNIS ET CANADA : M. le Prof. J. R. Workman, Brown University, Providence 12, Rhode Island.

ESPAGNE : J.-M. Blázquez, Instituto de Arqueologia, 4, Duque de Medinaceli, Madrid.

FRANCE : M. J. Heurgon, Membre de l'Acad. des Inscr. et Belles-Lettres, Le Verger, Allée de la Pavillonne, 78170 – La-Celle-St-Cloud.

GRANDE-BRETAGNE : M. le Prof. Fergus Millar, Dept. of History, University College of London, Gower Street, London WC1E 6BT.

ITALIE : Mlle M. L. Paladini, 13, Via Bellotti, Milano.

PAYS-BAS : M. le Dr. K. H. E. Schutter, 6, Sloetstraat, Nimègue.

SUÈDE : M; le Prof. G. Saefflund, 52, 1 tr. Vasagatan, 11120, Sotckholm.

SUISSE : M. A. Cattin, 14, Grand-Rue, Cormondrèche (Neuchâtel), Suisse.

IMPRIMERIE UNIVERSA, B-9200 WETTEREN (BELGIQUE)

Classical Library

COLLECTION LATOMUS
Fondée par Marcel RENARD
VOLUME 172

Pervigilium Veneris

Edited with a Translation
and a Commentary
by

Laurence CATLOW

LATOMUS
REVUE D'ÉTUDES LATINES
60, RUE COLONEL CHALTIN
BRUXELLES
1980

EX BIBL. UNIV. EDINBURGEN.

Parentibus optimis
floreat ver suum in aeternum

D/1980/0415/89
√ISBN 2-87031-112-5

Droits de traduction, de reproduction et d'adaptation réservés pour tous pays.
Toute reproduction d'un extrait quelconque, par quelque procédé que ce soit et notamment par photocopie ou microfilm, est strictement interdite.

ACKNOWLEDGMENTS

My thanks are due to Peter Dronke, of Clare Hall, Cambridge, who supervised my preparation of the thesis from which this study sprang, to Guy Lee, of St. John's College, Cambridge, who read an early draft of the thesis and made many valuable suggestions, and to Allan Hood, of the University of Edinburgh, who has read and criticised several sections of this work. Professor Alan Cameron, of King's College, London, and Dr. Michael Lapidge of Clare Hall, were most helpful examiners, and Professor Cameron has generously allowed me access to his as yet unpublished work on the date and authorship of the *Pervigilium* ; the fact that we reach very different conclusions should not conceal the extent to which I have found his work stimulating and helpful. I feel a special debt of gratitude to Professor Otto Skutsch, of University College, London, who not only guided and inspired my fumbling efforts as an undergraduate before I had even read the *Pervigilium Veneris*, but was also unstinting in the help he bestowed upon my attempts to make sense of the MSS tradition of the *P.V.* His rigorous and sometimes pungent criticism has benefited many other sections of this study. The faults and limitations of this edition, of course, remain my own.

Sedbergh.

SIGLA

S = Codex Salmasianus Parisinus 10318, saec. VIII[2]
T = Codex Thuaneus Parisinus 8071, saec. IX/X
V = Codex Vindobonensis 9401, saec. XVI
A = Codex Ambrosianus S 81 sup., saec. XVI

   Following my conclusions on the MSS relationships the readings of A
are excluded from my *apparatus criticus*. For a full list of A's variants cf.
Cazzaniga (1955) 98-101, in which, together with many other errors, the
reading *lusit*, at line 29, is incorrectly attributed to A instead of V.

The MSS Tradition

That the MSS of the *Pervigilium* all derive from a single archetype is beyond doubt ; equally certain is that T, V and A form a separate branch of the stemma, a fact demonstrated by related or identical corruptions in lines 11, 17 and 23 where S is correct (for TV alone cf. also lines 55, 62, 69, 78, 82, 86, 87 and 91). That T and A are more intimately related to each other than to V is shown by shared errors in 3, 9, 10, 32 and by their omission of 40, *loci* where V preserves the correct readings with S [1].

The value of S as an independent witness to the archetype is unassailable, whereas A, as I shall prove below, is a worthless copy of T. Argument centres upon the place of V in the MSS tradition of the *Pervigilium*, for this manuscript is a copy of a now missing original made by the poet and scholar Sannazaro in the early years of the sixteenth century [2] ; it is a far more accurate manuscript than its more venerable relative T, an accurary which might be explained by any of the following propositions : i) that although V descends from T it has been influenced by S or a MS of the same family as S, notably in its restoration of the correct readings in 9-10 and by its inclusion of 40 which had dropped out of T (the view of Schenkl [3] and Cazzaniga), ii) that V's accuracy may in

---

(1) The preservation of the *P.V.* in *Vind.* 9401 was first noticed by K. SCHENKL (*Zeit. für die österreichischen Gymnasien*, XXII (1871), 127-8, although the MS is incorrectly cited as 9041). The *codex* is a collection of disparate material ; the relevant section is found in folios 29-43 consisting of 56 poems from the Latin Anthology, including the *P.V.*, with the superscription *Epigrammata quaedam vetusta ab Actio Sincerio Sannazario exscripta*. In a later article Schenkl ('Zu lateinischen Anthologie' *WS* (1879), 59-62) published a list of V's contents and its variant readings. For a brief discussion of V's general contents, other than the *P.V.*, cf. the concluding paragraph of this chapter.

(2) Within the years 1501-4 during Sannazaro's exile in France. For the certain fact that the transcript is the work of Sannazaro, cf. Sir Cyril CLEMENTI, *The Pervigilium Veneris*[3] (London, 1936), 42-5.

(3) Cf. SCHENKL (1879) 59, on *Vind.* 9401 in general : 'Der Codex stimmt meistens mit dem Parisinus 8071', after which Schenkl mentions the fact that V has many readings common to S. 'Wir haben also hier, wie ich schon hinsichtlich des Pervigilium Veneris bemerkt habe, eine gemischte Recension, wie sich denn auch Lesearten von A und B

large part be the result of Sannazarian conjecture (Schilling and Rand ([4]),
iii) that V reflects an earlier stage of the stemmatic tradition than T
(Valgiglio) ([5]).

The text of V is not consistent with i), for if Sannazaro's original was a
descendant of T, Sannazaro himself, or an earlier copyist, must have been
familiar with S (or a related MS) and must have used this knowledge to
restore line 40, suitably emended, and to correct lines 9-10. Why then has
S exerted such a local influence and not been used to correct, for example,
Dione in line 11, *decadum punder* in 17, *fusta* in 23, *Latino* in 69 or *an
tacendo* in 91 ? No doubt plausible circumstances could be conjectured to
explain the haphazard nature of this supposed process, but scholarly
debate upon the *Pervigilium*, indeed widespread knowledge of the poem's
existence ([6]), followed only after the publication of Pithou's *editio princeps*

(Thuaneus) neben einander finden'. This must mean that, in Schenkl's opinion, V belongs
to the same tradition as T or derives from T but has been partially corrected with reference
to S. Baehrens (*P.L.M.* IV, 9) is unequivocal : *'ex B fluxerunt Epigrammata quaedam ab
Actio Sincerio Sannazario exscripta in cod. Vind. 9041'* (note the incorrect citation
inherited from Schenkl and bequeathed to Riese, who, in his introduction to the *A.L.*
(Leipzig, 1894) XXXVII, follows Baehrens' pronouncement on V). Elsewhere in this
introduction (XIII) he suggests that V's agreement with S should be explained, not by the
influence of S itself, but by Sannazaro's correction of 9401 from the archetype of T. Cf.
my discussion of *Cod. Vind.* 277 *infra*).

(4) R. SCHILLING, *La Veillée de Vénus* (Paris, 1944), LXIII ; E. K. RAND, in his review of
Clementi's *P.V., AJPh* LVIII (1937), 474-8.

(5) E. VALGIGLIO, 'Sulla tradizione manoscritta del *P.V.*', *BPEC* XV (1967), 115-35.
Valgiglio takes the trouble to prove that V does not derive from S (116-17), a fact which is
not in doubt, but does not bother to consider Cazzaniga's argument that V is a version of T
corrected from S. The study is marred throughout by Valgiglio's treatment of purely
orthographical variants as transmitted readings, and by the assumption that errors
peculiar to particular MSS almost inevitably derive from manuscript forbears rather than
spontaneous scribal error, or attempted emendation.

(6) The earliest reference to the *P.V.* occurs in the 2nd edition of Erasmus' *Adagia*
(published in 1508) *chilias* I, 820 :*meminit de Amyclarum silentio Silius Italicus : 'quasque
evertere silentia Amyclae'. meminit et Catullus, nisi fallit inscriptio carminis DE VERE
quod nuper Aldus Manutius meus exhibuit, in antiquissima Galliae bibliotheca repertum :
'sic Amyclas, dum tacebant, perdidit silentium'.* (quoted by Clementi, p. 4). Manutius and
Erasmus, both men of learning, obviously encountered the *Pervigilium* in a context of
total ignorance concerning its name, nature and very existence.

Clementi believed that the discovery of the Manutian MS might mark a great step
forward towards accurate restoration of the text. He lists the following reasons in favour
of its importance (p. 7) : 'a) because the penultimate line of the poem as quoted by
Erasmus differs from the text in S, T and V ; b) because S, T and V do not ascribe the
poem to Catullus ; c) because in S, T and V the poem is expressly titled *Pervigilium
Veneris* which cannot have been the case with the MS Erasmus and Manuzio saw ; and

in 1577, an edition based on T alone, while the *codex Salmasianus* itself seems to have done little more active than gather dust until its discovery by Salmasius in the early 17th century ([7]). Against this background of obscurity, and given the state of the text in V, it is most unlikely that its inclusion of line 40, or the accurate preservation of 9-10, stems from any MS other than the missing original which Sannazaro copied. This MS cannot, therefore, have been a descendant of T.

But, if Sannazaro's MS belonged to the same family as T, but was independent of T itself, should V's substantial accuracy be attributed (*marginalia* apart) to faithful transmission or to emendation ? The very scale of V's agreement with S, where T is corrupt, suggests that this accuracy is archetypal, an impression confirmed by the consideration that V shares with T many errors which cry out for simple and obvious emendation. A scholar who could correct *pudent* to *pudebit* (26), *acuneo* to *arcu neu* (33), *fluctus* to *fluxit* (61), and *adsonante aerii* to *adsonat Terei* (86) ([8]), would surely have been able to see *Dionem* in *Dione* (11), *comes* in *comis* (29), *Latinos* in *Latino* (69) or *tutus* in *tuus* (82), to mention only a few instances where V begs for correction but remains corrupt. Moreover, assuming that V is a heavily corrected version of the tradition represented by T, nowhere does the process of emendation seem to have introduced further corruption through misinterpretation or false conjecture. These features form a significant contrast with the editorial work of Pithou and Scaliger ([9]). Working from T alone they have purged the text

finally d) because the poem in S, T and V begins with the refrain and not with the line *ver novum* etc.' (on the assumption that Erasmus' description, *carmen de vere*, derives from the first line of Manutius' text).

But these arguments prove only that the Manutian MS was neither S, T or V, not that it was independent. The variant reading mentioned in a) could easily stem from emendation of T, moreover b) clearly points to the influence of T for in T Catullus 62 precedes the *P.V.* with only a short interval and the superscription to Cat. 62 (*Epithalamium Catulli*) may have been misinterpreted by a copyist of T and applied to a whole group of poems including the *P.V.* Both c) and d) are examples of omission which cannot be regarded as evidence for independence. The evidence of b) suggests that the MS of Erasmus and Manutius was a corrupt descendant of T, which completely dominated the scholarship of the *P.V.* until the belated appearance of S.

(7) For the prolonged obscurity, eventual discovery, and subsequent history of S, cf. RIESE (1894) XII-VIII.

(8) Some of T's errors, of course, will have been the innovations of its scribe, but, if V is a heavily emended MS, then its original would have shared T's corruption in many, if not all, of these instances.

(9) For the conjectures of Pithou and Scaliger, cf. H. OMONT, 'Conjectures de J. Scaliger sur le *P.V.*', *RPh* IX (1885), 124-6.

of those obvious blemishes which are faithfully preserved in V. Moreover
Pithou has brilliantly perceived that *inermis* should be *in armis* while,
metri causa, Scaliger has restored *praeses* in 50. But there are occasions
where their assault upon corruption leads away from, not towards, the
truth. Note Pithou's version of line 9 :

> *Juno rore de supernis spumeo ponti e globo*

and observe how Scaliger 'corrects' and rearranges 22-5 :

> *ipsa iussit mane tutae virgines ludant. Rosae*
> *fusae Amoris de cruore deque Adonis osculis,*
> *deque gemmis deque flammis deque solis purpuris*
> *in pudorem florulentae prodierunt purpurae.*

   The extent, then, of V's agreement with S, its retention of simple errors
which serious attention from Sannazaro, or an earlier scholar, must surely
have removed, and the further consideration that it is free from the bold
but often misleading innovations which are such a feature of humanist
scholarship ([10]) at work with unsatisfactory MSS, all lead me to the
confident conclusion that V's accuracy is *in large measure* due to faithful
transmission from the archetype, and that V therefore represents an
earlier stage of the MSS tradition than T. But there are several *loci* where S
and T agree in error against the correct reading in V. Some of these
mistakes may have occurred independently (e.g. *tumentis* in 16 – through
dittography), but others obviously reflect corruption at a very early stage
before the stemma had split ([11]). In such instances V's readings must be the
result of unattested emendation in the main text. MSS were, of course,
exposed to silent correction at all stages of their transmission, and the very
limited evidence for this process in the text of V does not seriously
challenge my estimate of its importance : as the nearest witness to the
intermediary archetype from which T and A also derive, and thus,
together with S, our chief source for the state of the archetype common to
all the MSS.

---

   (10) Cf. note 17 for a discussion of Sannazaro's editorial work on the *Halieutica* and
the *Cynegeticon* and the contrast this forms with his treatment of the *P.V.*
   (11) Cf. *App. Crit.* at lines 16, 52, 54, 62, 65, 92. Purely orthographical variants are not
considered.

Marginal and interlinear corrections

V contains a number of corrections in the margin which are almost certainly Sannazarian conjectures ([12]) and which are admitted as such into my apparatus. Relatively scarce and generally simple but convincing corrections of obvious MS corruption, they are more significant in the light they shed on Sannazaro's method of transcription than as a notable advance in the scholarship of the *Pervigilium*. For since Sannazaro has bothered to record *posuit* as a correction for *possuit* (31) and *iussitque* for *iusitque* (67), I find it difficult to believe that he would have introduced more ambitious emendations in the main text without marginal advertisement. This forces the very welcome conclusion that he devoted very little intellectual effort upon his work on the *Pervigilium*, that he must have regarded his function as that of a copyist rather than a scholar, merely noting marginally simple corrections as they occurred to him.

The same conclusion follows from consideration of the interlinear insertions ([13]). It has not been realised that these cannot represent the work of Sannazaro himself, for it is inconceivable that *unicat* (26) should recommend itself to him as better Latin than *unica*, that he should prefer *virgentes* to *vigentes* (58) (indeed the marginal *vigentibus virentes* proves that he thought *virgentes* corrupt), or that he should suggest *furta* for *fusta* in a context where both are equally meaningless (23). Clearly, while the marginal corrections represent Sannazaro's work on the text, interlinear

---

(12) Marginal emendation is accompanied by the abbreviation f., except at 67 (*iussitque* for *iusitque*), where its omission is probably an oversight, and at line 52, where the marginal *restem* is, in fact, not an emendation but clarifies the obscured line-reading. Clementi (p. 46) believed that f. stands for *fortasse* but, as Cazzaniga points out, some of Sannazaro's conjectures are so certain that he would scarcely have proposed them with such circumspection. More convincing is Schilling's proposal that f. = *fiat* (p. LXII n.).

Cazzaniga himself suggests that marginal comment does not necessarily represent Sannazarian conjecture at all but Sannazarian collation, and that f. may indicate the source of these variant readings. On this assumption it seems apposite to wonder why collation has only occurred in cases of obvious, single-word corruption, and not where V poses real problems. Far more likely is that marginal comment, as has generally been assumed, consists of simple emendations which occurred to Sann. in the process of transcription. It is, of course, possible that the *marginalia* were already present in Sann.'s original MS. In this case their preservation, as Valgiglio points out (p. 119), would be evidence of Sann.'s scrupulous accuracy as a copyist, for many of the marginal suggestions are so obviously correct that most scribes would have silently incorporated them into their main text.

(13) Cf. *App. Crit.* 9, 15, 23, 26, 39, 58.

comment was already present in his original MS ([14]). Sannazaro's incorporation of these features therefore constitutes a further indication that his transcription is a faithful reflection of its parent, while their very scarcity suggests that his original had not received undue attention from reforming scholars.

THE ORIGINAL OF V

V is a faithful copy of a MS which was nearer the archetype than T. This inevitably raises the possibility that Sannazaro's original was either the immediate or more remote ancestor of T itself. The relationship between the MSS might, in fact, be the precise opposite of that proposed by Cazzaniga.

Such an eventuality is in no way precluded by the few instances where T preserves the correct reading against corruption in V (cf. *App. Crit.* to 21, 28, 31, 38, 47, 67); all these cases are perfectly consistent with the assumption of T's dependence upon V's parent, for the scribe of T, as Richmond ([15]) has shown, was subject to an erratic urge to correct the readings of the MS he was copying. He would not, it is true, have emended *virgines* to *virgineas*, but V's error here might plausibly be attributed to a Sannazarian misreading.

Particularly interesting, in the context of this possibility, is Schenkl's proof that, with the exception of Juvenal's *Satires*, all the material of T was copied from a late-eighth or early-ninth century MS of which two quires (numbered 17 and 18) still survive as part of *Cod. Vind.* 277 ([16]). It was from this MS that Sannazaro, during his exile, made two copies of both the ps.-Ovidian *Halieutica* and of Grattius' *Cynegeticon* ([17]). *Vind.*

---

(14) At 39 correction in the line is accompanied by marginal clarification, *nemus*, which could, therefore, be regarded as a Sannazarian conjecture, but since he has not elsewhere accompanied marginal correction with interlinear alteration, it is more likely that the reading *venus* is from his original and that Sann. has marginally added *nemus* to obviate confusion.

(15) J. A. RICHMOND, *Halieutica* (London, 1962) 7-8.

(16) H. SCHENKL, 'Zur Kritik und Überlieferungsgeschichte des Grattius und anderer lateinischer Dichter', *JKPh* suppl. XXIV (1898) 399-400.

(17) For a discussion of these apographs, cf. H. SCHENKL (1898), 387-92, who includes their readings in his apparatus to the *Halieutica* and the *Cynegeticon*. They illustrate Sannazaro's serious work as an editor, and display a quite different approach from his treatment of the *P.V.* The earlier copy of the two poems shows a marked tendency for bold emendations *even where the text is not in need of alteration*, while the second version is the fruit of painstaking scholarship (cf. Schenkl, 390-1). A glance at Schenkl's apparatus

277 is the parent of T, when complete it preserved the *Pervigilium*, it was a MS with which Sannazaro was certainly familiar. In such circumstances it is at least worth asking, as does Schenkl himself and in a manner which invites a positive response [18], whether *Vind*. 277 still contained the *P.V.* when discovered by Sannazaro and whether it was his source for *Vind*. 9401 as for his copies of the *Halieutica* and *Cynegeticon*. Is V a faithful transcription of the MS which the scribe of T has copied with such carelessness [19] ?

I at first assumed that this must be the case, but further reflection has changed my thinking on this question which I now answer negatively. Two considerations seem conclusive to me. Firstly the fact that Schenkl's argument demonstrates that T is not only a descendant, but a direct copy of *Vind*. 277 [20]. How, then, have Sannazaro and the scribe of T produced such radically different versions of the same MS, notably at lines 9-10, when all the evidence suggests that Sannazaro himself worked swiftly, more as a copyist than an editor ? Perhaps more decisive are the corruptions shared by S and T in lines 52, 54, 62 and 65, where V is correct ; these can scarcely have originated independently, and must represent archetypal error which has been removed from V by emendation. The fact that this emendation is unaccompanied by marginal comment almost certainly means that it was pre-Sannazarian and already present in his source for V. This MS, therefore, cannot have been *Vind*. 277, which must have preserved the archetypal corruptions it has bequeathed to T.

clearly demonstrates that Sann.'s second attempt upon the text of these difficult poems reflects an effort of intellect and concentration of an altogether separate order from his attentions to the *P.V.*, while the earlier copy, with unwanted conjecture a conspicuous feature, is equally remote from the faithful preservation of MS error in V.

(18) P. 400, quoted in note (19).

(19) No editor of the *P.V.* has seriously considered this possibility. Clementi (p. 40) is aware of Schenkl's article, but not of its implications and, after the briefest of discussions, merely discards *Vind*. 277 as a possible source of V : 'it is quite likely that Sannazaro, during his sojourn in France, made from yet another MS, the copy of the *P.V.* ... now preserved in V'. He makes no mention of Schenkl's estimate of 9401 (p. 400) : 'seine (i.e. Sannazaro's) Abschrift der Anthologie-Exzerpte weicht bekanntermassen vom Thuaneus in nicht unerheblichen Weise ab und zeigt bessere Lesarten, die man gewöhnlich einer flüchtigen Einsicht in den Salmasianus zuschreibt. Wie, wenn diese Vorzüge nur darauf beruhten, das Sannazar das Original und nicht die Copie benutzte ?'

(20) Schenkl's reconstruction of the contents of *Vind*. 277 is based on a study of the pagination of 277 and T. His conclusions can only mean that T is immediately derived from the older MS. I cannot, therefore, allow Richmond's imprecise claim (p. 7) 'that T is an immediate or *more remote* ancestor of B' (Thuaneus).

The evidence of lines 52, 54, 62 and 65 proves that Sannazaro's original cannot have been a direct ancestor of T ; the evidence of V in general suggests that his MS was a sparsely emended and accurate copy, probably at one remove, of an ancient manuscript which via subsequent careless transcriptions and finally through the agency of *Vind*. 277, was the source of the *P.V.* as preserved in T.

COD. AMBROSIANUS S 81 SUPPL.

The close affinity between the text of the *P.V.* in T and A is explained quite simply by Cazzaniga : A is a descendant of T spasmodically corrected by humanist conjecture. But Valgiglio [21], while admitting that A 'non da nessun apporto concreto alla constitutione del testo', nevertheless argues that A is an independent MS, derived, not from T, but from a common ancestor. He does not say whether he means *Vind*. 277 by this MS or an earlier stage in the transmission. The principal reason for Valgiglio's defence of A is agreement between A and V where T is corrupt [22], an agreement he believes to reflect transmission rather than emendation of the A text.

The matter can fortunately be settled by a brief glance at the contents of A other than the *P.V.*, for it also contains parts of the *Halieutica* and the *Cynegeticon* [23], material still preserved in both Thuaneus and *Vind*. 277 ; and Schenkl has shown how the numerous instances of agreement between A and T against the readings of *Vind*. 277 prove that A is derived from Thuaneus, not from the old Vindobonensis. Where A is correct and T in error, this reflects the endeavours of humanist scholarship.

It would be absurd to claim that A has copied the *Halieutica* from T, but the *Pervigilium* from *Vind*. 277 or a still earlier MS, unless the nature of the text demanded so involved an interpretation. Since, therefore, the preservation of the *P.V.* in A is entirely consistent with Schenkl's argument, I have no doubt that A's text of the *Pervigilium*, as too of the *Halieutica* and the *Cynegeticon*, is derived from T with the inclusion of some humanist conjectures [24].

---

(21) VALGIGLIO, 123-4, for Cazzaniga's argument cf. 85ff.

(22) Excluding orthographical variants this occurs at lines 1-5, 8, 13, 16-19, 20-2, 24, 28, 33 (twice), 36, 38, 39, 41. In all these instances (cf. *App. Crit. ad loc.*) the accuracy of A is explicable in terms of simple emendation.

(23) Cf. SCHENKL (1898), 394-6.

(24) Cazzaniga, and Valgiglio himself, both point to several *loci* where the readings of

The Codex Ambrosianus represents a half-hearted attempt to purify the tradition of T prior to the attention of serious scholars such as Pithou, Scaliger and Statius. Its sole value lies in the fact that, by illustrating all those glaring faults which V so commendably lacks, it can only exalt our opinion of V as in independent witness to the text. Wherever faced by substantial difficulty A makes a bad text worse through conjecture. It points away from, not towards the truth, for even when its emendation of serious corruption in T is not patently absurd, the result is still the same : that the genuine reading has become less not more accessible. I am sure that, faced with T or one of its progeny, Sannazaro could have made better sense of it than the scribe of A, but, considering the nature of A, and comparing this with the very different condition of the text in V, let us reject once for all Cazzaniga's false assertion that A and V share a common ancestor in T. V is an important, independent MS, A is a worthless copy of T.

FURTHER CONTENTS OF V

My conclusions about the nature and value of V as a witness to the text of the *Pervigilium* are supported by the state of the other poems which it preserves [25]. Contrary to the statement of Schenkl, all its fifty six poems are also found in T, where they appear in substantially the same order [26]. Throughout V there are many errors shared with T where S is correct, and many correct readings in common with S where T is corrupt [27].

A clearly reflect an unequal struggle to extract some meaning from T's nonsense (*qui vere* for *quivore* in 9, *dea dum* for *decadum* in 17), while *pudet dissolvere* in 26 is an attempt to repair the disruption of sense and metre in T (*pudent solvere*). These are places where the copyist-editor of A has encountered corruption too deep-seated for him to cope with, but, against the background of this conjectural endeavour, the assumption that the correct readings which A shares with V derive from transmission rather than emendation, is highly questionable, even apart from the arguments advanced above.

(25) V's variants are catalogued by K. SCHENKL (1879) 59-62. I have followed him in referring to poems as numbered in Riese's edition of the *Anthologia*.

(26) SCHENKL (1879) 61, refers to 'vier bisher unbekannte Epigramme', but these too are preserved by T, cf. BÄHRENS, *P.L.M.* IV, 9.

(27) For corruption with T against the correct text in S, cf. 111, 1, *sexu* (TV), *flexu* (S) ; 129, 5, *utrumque* (TV), *utroque* S ; 131, 3, *tunc cocum iubeas tupeas* (TV), *trunco cum stupeas* (S). These are just random examples of a constantly recurring phenomenon, as are the following instances of V in agreement with S where T is corrupt : 101, 5 *ne per* (SV), *nec per* (T) ; 117, 1 *amictu* (SV), *comictu* (T) ; 129, 2, *clune* (SV), *dune* (T).

Marginal and interlinear correction is about as frequent as in the text of the *P.V.* My argument that interlinear alteration cannot be the work of Sannazaro seems to be confirmed by 183, 1, where 'n' is inserted above the final letter of *fex* (= *faex*), an innovation which could not have suggested itself to Sannazaro, and by 192, 3, where the orthography of *scriptorum* is 'improved' by the insertion of a 'b' over the 'p'. This can only reflect Sannazaro's faithful transcription of his original. Generally speaking interlinear work seems to reflect two opposite processes ; sometimes the scribe has copied MS corruption and then suggested his emendation above the text (cf. line 9 of *P.V.* ; 197, 9 *cursus*, *cursus* ST) ; on other occasions he has emended the text, and then inserted the reading of his MS. This is the case at 197, 4, where the apparent (and certainly correct) emendation *astra* appears in the main text below the inserted *atra* (ST) [28]. Similarly at 251, 2 the line-ending *quam malum est semper pudor* appears to be an (again correct) emendation of the reading in S (*quam malum est per pudor*) which V preserves in the margin. At 250, 1 we find the corrupt reading of T (*offugia*, *officia* S) immediately followed in the main text by the certain emendation *offucias*. This reading also appears as a marginal correction in S, but is not necessarily evidence, as Schenkl suggests, for mixed recension : the correction in S is probably the work of Saumaise and would thus appear in S only after V had been copied [29]. We appear to be dealing here with independent correction.

I have already, with specific regard to the *P.V.*, pointed to places in V where unattested emendation seems to have occurred. 117, 8 (*lascivis* for *lascibus* S, *lascivius* T), 181, 9 (*peremptae* for *peremit* S, *parente* T), and 216, 10 (*chelis* (= *chelys*) for *caelis* ST) confirm my impression that the tradition representend by V has at some stage been spasmodically emended by a scribe who did not take the trouble to indicate his corrections. The instances given above might conceivably be examples of correct transmission, where S and T have introduced independent errors. No such doubt attends 197, 6, where V reads *urguet* against *habet* in S and *aptet* in T. 117, 21 represents a far bolder attempt to make sense out of nonsense, for there we find in V :

> *arva November arans fecundo vomere vertit,*

(28) Schenkl's comment that here is a place where, 'sich ... Lesearten von A und B neben einander finden', is mistaken : *atra* is the reading of both S and T, *astra* of neither.

(29) Saumaise cannot have been shown S before 1609 (cf. RIESE, intro. XIV), whereas Sannazaro copied V over a century earlier.

whereas S and T transmit *arat* (*arans* T) *fecundo nomine bestiae*. I cannot believe with Riese (cf. *App. Crit.*) that Sannazaro would have introduced such a drastic innovation without some form of marginal announcement, and I am frankly puzzled by the state of V here.

If, after our discussion of the text of the *P.V.*, the fact that V is not a descendant of T is still felt to require proof, then further evidence is at hand, for at 129, 1 V preserves *nomen* with S, a word which T omits. The V-text all around bristles with corruptions shared with T but not S. In such a context it is absurd to talk of collation and unlikely that the text of V derives from anything but its original, which cannot therefore have been T. Another interesting reading occurs at 101, 2, where S and V both read *palatum*, while V offers marginally the reading of T (*patulum*). If V derives from T then *patulum* should be in the text not in the margin. It is probable, moreover, that V here explains the origin of the text in T, for the marginal *patulum* is probably pre-Sannazarian ([30]) and probably existed in the margin of an earlier MS whence the T tradition has absorbed it into the main text. 113, 5 also shows V preserving an earlier stage of the transmission than T ([31]), for there V's *namque itae quali* is virtually identical with *namque ita aequali* in S. The text in T (*nam lira aequali*), with the disappearance of *que* and the metamorphosis of an adverb into a musical instrument (or ridge of earth) ([32]), marks a further process of corruption. It is, I think, unnecessary to multiply arguments in favour of a thesis which emerges as self-evident from an impartial examination of the evidence : that V is not only independent of T but, except where it has been emended, preserves an earlier stage of the branch of the MSS tradition which culminates with, or rather degenerates into, T and A.

(30) Since it is accompanied, not by the customary sign f., but by the mark f̂.
(31) Note too 111, 5, *graia* (SV) against the correct *grata* of T, where S and V preserve an error which has been emended out of T ; unless V and S have made the same mistake independently.
(32) Sense suggests the lyre, metre the ridge of earth !

Date and Authorship

DATE

That the *Pervigilium Veneris* was written in the post-classical era of Latin literature is beyond doubt. No modern editor has attempted to prove otherwise, and Erasmus obviously regarded the ascription to Catullus, in his MS of the *Pervigilium*, with deep suspicion [1]. Here unanimity ends and editors split into two broad factions which enthusiastically champion rival centuries, the second and the fourth, as the period to which the *Pervigilium* belongs [2].

The earlier date is normally supported by appeal to the promotion of the cult of *Venus Genetrix* undertaken by Hadrian [3], and some more ambitious scholars have even indicated that the poem was composed for, or inspired by, a specific occasion : Hadrian's state-visit to Sicily in 123 [4]. But there is nothing in the *Pervigilium* to suggest that it is the work of a court poet [5] and it is certainly not a genuinely liturgical poem. Nor is there any evidence that celebration of the birth of Venus, the event which the *Pervigilium* commemorates, was a feature of Hadrian's religious policy. The cult worship of *Venus genetrix* fostered by Hadrian clearly exalted her special relationship to the Roman people as the mother of Aeneas, and glorified the Roman state by honouring the goddess so

---

(1) *Adag. chil*. I, 820, on the proverb *Amyclas perdidit silentium*, cf. 'the MSS Tradition', note (6).

(2) The attribution of the poem to Seneca (VON BARTH 1624), the suggestion that the *P.V.* is a humanist fraud (CABARET-DUPATY 1624), and the proposal that it is the fruit of poetic collaboration between a man and his wife (WERNSDORF 1782) are too absurd to deserve detailed rejection, as too is BOUHIER's (1720) fancy that the poem represents a conflation of two works of widely different date. Theories of date and authorship based upon line 74 are dealt with separately in the notes *ad loc*. and are almost certainly based on misinterpretation of the line.

(3) As, for example, by SCHILLING XXIV-V.

(4) Notably LATKOCZY (1894), whose proposal is accepted in a modified form, by BOYANCÉ (1966), 1560-3.

(5) Cf. notes to line 74.

intimately involved with Rome's destiny [6]. But, in the *Pervigilium*, Venus' imperial rôle is unmentioned until line 69 and the stanza which deals with this is the least impressive in the whole poem. The *Pervigilium Veneris* praises Venus as queen of the heart ; under her influence the thoughts of the virgin turn to love and marriage, the festival is to culminate in the initiation of these virgins into the mysteries of love : this points away from, not towards, an imperial court. Hadrian's advancement of the worship of Venus as a central feature of Roman state-religion is thus of no significance as an indication of an appropriate period for the composition of the *Pervigilium Veneris*.

The argument in favour of the fourth century is more solidly based upon the evidence of style and vocabulary ; but before examining this I would prefer to deal with some of the impressionistic nonsense that has been written about the metrical tendencies and stylistic flavour of the *Pervigilium*. We have been told (by Fort (1922), for example) that the *P.V.* exemplifies a transitional phase between classical and medieval metrical practice in that the poet cultivates coincidence between the stress of pronunciation and the ictus of metre. This is simply untrue ; conflict between accent and ictus is a constant feature of the *P.V.*, and Tiberianus' *Amnis ibat* is far further along the road towards metrical and accentual harmony. If this were our sole criterion for dating the *Pervigilium*, I would place it nearer Seneca than Tiberianus (cf. my fuller treatment at pp. 40-42).

Again we have been told that the *P.V.*, even apart from the metre, *sounds* unclassical. Pater's treatment of the poem in *Marius the Epicurean* is the *locus classicus* for this view (cf. pp. 73-85) ; his evocation of the *P.V.*, as a sort of prelude to the poetry of the Middle Ages, is used extensively by Clementi in the introduction to his edition of the poem, and Wilhelm (1965, 20f.) attempts to analyse the new laws of sound which the poet has formulated. In so far as these claims about the sound of the *Pervigilium* mean anything, they must mean that the poet's love of assonance points to the Middle Ages rather than to the classical poets ; and I do not understand this. Our poet is particularly found of accumulating 'O' sounds ; this is an idiosyncrasy which imparts a full-bodied flavour to many of his lines. But, apart from this, I can identify no marked tendency

---

(6) Hadrian's dedication of the *Templum Veneris et Romae* (cf. *RE* Venus III, 20) emphasizes the nature of his religious policy : *Venus genetrix* is a purely political conception ; of politics or propaganda there is no hint in the *P.V.*.

towards internal or end rhyme, nothing but the rich and varied interplay between sonorous textures of sound which is a glory of Latin poetry in the era of Catullus and Virgil no less, and perhaps more, than in the medieval period.

The evidence for a date well into the post-classical period consists of details. The general feel and flavour of the *P.V.* have, in this context, nothing to tell us. Brakman ([7]) instanced the use of *vel* as a synonym for *et*, the regular employment of *praesens pro futuro* (cf. Leum. II, 307-8), the lengthening of the short third syllabe of *Romuleus* (72), the choice of the post-classical adjective *congrex* (43), and the poet's partiality for the preposition *de*, as a cumulative indication of a date not earlier than the middle of the fourth century. But the copulative use of *vel* is classical and *congrex* appears as early as Apuleius. In fact the vocabulary of the *Pervigilium* does not yield very much ; although *florulentus* (19) and *copulatrix* (5) do not emerge elsewhere before the fourth century, they are not striking innovations; while the poets fondness for well-established graecisms suggests no specific period of post-classical antiquity.

Far more significant is the false quantity in *Romuleus*. The MS, although not the editions, of Tiberianus' *Amnis ibat*, preserves an even harsher lengthening at line seven :

> *et nemus fragrabat omne violarum spiritu.*

Baehren's insertion of *sub* before *spiritu* is the simplest of the various conjectures, and emendation is perhaps necessary (incidentally Baehrens, who identifies Tiberianus as the author of the *Pervigilium*, should have proposed *de*), but, even without this striking parallel, such a violation of prosody, in the work of so literate a poet, is far more typical of fourth than of second century practice. The most telling feature of style, however, because it can be exactly parallelled, is the poet's use of *de*, an affectation the poet shares only with Augustine and Fulgentius in their popular psalms, which thus suggests that we are dealing with a feature of late-African Latinity ([8]).

And yet the poet's *choice* of metre is as suggestive as any of these considerations ; for, beyond three passages in Senecan tragedy which are clearly directly inspired by Greek models, the tetrameter is almost, if not

---

(7) C. Brakman, 'Quando *Pervigilium Veneris* conditum est', *Mnemosyne* LVI (1928) 254-70.

(8) Cf. notes to line 4.

completely, neglected by Roman poets before the fourth century (cf. further pp. 36-7). The eight short poems in tetrameters, preserved as *A.L.* 245-52, cannot be dated with any certainty (cf. p. 21-2), but in the fourth century the tetrameter suddenly blossoms as a lyric metre, when it is taken to the service of the Church by Hilary and Prudentius and finds a secular exponent in Tiberianus. This is the beginning of a great tradition, and it is this which, together with the metrical and stylistic details discussed above, persuades me that the *P.V.* is more at home in the fourth than in the second century, and that a date of composition after 350 is more likely than one before.

AUTHORSHIP

The name most frequently associated with the authorship of the *Pervigilium Veneris* has been that of Florus, an intimate of the emperor Hadrian, an historian as well as a poet, who has generally been identified with the Florus to whom the *codex Salmasianus* attributes a handful of poems in the *Anthologia Latina* ([9]). The arguments in favour of a fourth-century date are not final and would be outweighed by substantial evidence in favour of an earlier poet. This is not the case with Florus, whose claim has been based by editors upon two equally unconvincing arguments: his association with Hadrian and supposed similarities between his poetry and the *Pervigilium*.

Florus' friendship with Hadrian is of no significance, since the connection of the *Pervigilium* with Hadrian's religious policy is falsely conceived, while Schilling's interpretation of the closing lines of the *Pervigilium* with reference to the biographical details preserved in the surviving fragment of Florus' *Virgilius, poeta an rhetor*, is a flight of fancy rather than a piece of serious scholarship. The circumstantial approach produces no cogent argument for uprooting the *Pervigilium* from the fourth century, a period suggested by all the more solid evidence at our disposal.

(9) Schilling XXII-XXXII ; O. Mueller, *De P. Annio Floro et Perv. Ven.* (Berlin, 1855) ; E. Laurenti, *De Iulio Annaeo Floro poeta atque historico P.V. auctore RFIC* XX (1892) 125-43 ; Rand, *REL* XII (1934) 90-5. Confusion over the *praenomen* and *nomen* stems from the MSS of different works, but it is not seriously doubted that the Florus of the *Epitome*, the Florus of *Virgilius, poeta an rhetor*, and the poet-friend of Hadrian are one and the same person ; whether he is also the Florus of the *A.L.* is another matter, as I point out below.

The argument from Florus' poetry rests solely upon those poems in the *Anthologia* which have come down to us under his name ([10]), and I find it surprising that the mere facts that *A.L.* 87 is a description of rose-blooms and that *A.L.* 245-252 are written in trochaic tetrameters should have left editors queuing up to claim Florus as the author of the *Pervigilium*. We should remember first of all that, of the two MSS which preserve *A.L.* 245-52, only *Salmasianus* attributes them to Florus (in *Thuaneus* the ascription is to a certain Floridus), while what guarantee can there be, even if a poet called Florus wrote these poems (together with *A.L.* 87), that he is to be identified with the Hadrianic poet of that name. And even if we persist in making this dangerous assumption, I can still see nothing to suggest that Florus might have written the *Pervigilium*. His tetrameters display features alien to the metrical practice of the poet of the *Pervigilium* ([11]), the 'symétries d'expression' which Schilling seeks to establish between *A.L.* 87 and the *P.V.* are either non-existent or depend upon doubtful emendation ([12]); and, above all, Florus' verse nowhere displays any hint of the genius which animates line after line of the *Pervigilium Veneris*. Is it good policy, in looking for the author of a great poem, to fasten upon a talent which was no better than second-rate ? It is with complete confidence that I reject Florus, who is anyway quite probably a composite figure, as a possible author of the *Pervigilium Veneris*.

Tiberianus is a more promising candidate, especially if he can be identified with the *vir disertus* mentioned in Jerome's chronicle as the governor of Gaul in A.D. 335, for the middle of the fourth century is a promising period for the scholar in search of our author. But the metrical affinities between his *Amnis ibat* and the *Pervigilium* ([13]) are more than outweighed by significant differences of usage, notably by the tendency in Tiberianus towards coincidence between metrical and accentual stress throughout the line, which is not apparent in the *Pervigilium*, and by Tiberianus' much freer admission of accumulations of purely trochaic feet. It is of course true that the same poet might easily use the same metre

---

(10) Cf. J. WIGHT DUFF, *Minor Latin Poets* (London, 1934) 423-35 for the collection of verse, which some editors have attributed to Florus. Of these poems only I is beyond doubt his work ; the attribution of II-X rests on the authority of the *cod. Salmasianus*, while the remainder are ascribed to Florus with no supporting authority or justification.

(11) Cf. 'the Metre', p. 40.

(12) Cf. SCHILLING, XXIX.

(13) Cf. 'the Metre', pp. 39-41.

differently on different occasions, but the argument in favour of
Tiberianus rests almost solely upon superficial metrical similarities
between the *Pervigilium* and the *Amnis ibat* ; in this context the far more
substantial divergences in practice must weigh against acceptance of his
authorship. Baehrens, who first championed the cause of Tiberianus [14],
emphasized the feeling for nature which animates both poems, but
whereas nature, in the *Amnis ibat*, is no more than a colourful and
charming landscape, it expresses, in the *Pervigilium*, a totally different
attitude as a vision of metaphysical truth.

Convinced that the *Pervigilium* belonged to the fourth century,
Brakman [15] was led by its blatant paganism to place its author among the
pagan circle of Q. Aurelius Symmachus. This theory has been accepted by
Rollo [16] who identifies the poet as Virius Nicomachus Flavianus, a
religious conservative who committed suicide in 393, whereas more
recently Herrmann [17] has suggested Claudius Antonius. The arguments
advanced in favour of one or other specific member of the Symmachean
coterie are based on the most trivial kind of circumstantial evidence, and
Brakman's broad thesis is open to the more general objection that, in spite
of its sentiments, the *Pervigilium* betrays no literary affinity with the
poetry of the circle of Symmachus ; for the Latinity of a Symmachus or an
Ausonius is, in their poetry at least, archaic and classicising, and
fastidiously avoids both the rhythms and phrasing of popular speech. And
yet the author of the *Pervigilium* deliberately affects a flagrantly vulgar
prepositional usage, a usage which Ausonius or Symmachus would surely
have regarded with shocked horror. Again the style of the *Pervigilium* is
generally direct and simple, its simplicity belonging to the simplicity of
great art. But the fashionable poetry of fourth century Roman society
delights in stylistic complexity, in elaborate and often unbearably tedious
decorative *topoi*, in irrelevant, exasperating and frequently inane displays
of scholarship, all of which are valued as ends in themselves. The author
of the *Pervigilium* was a poet of genius, it is true, which is more than can
be said of any of the known practitioners of the Symmachean circle, and
which would have helped him to avoid the idle preciosity which is so
typical of their work ; but, even given the assumption that in the

(14) Baehrens (1877), 36-7.
(15) Brakman (1928), 260-1.
(16) Rollo, *CPh* XXIV (1929) 405-8.
(17) Herrmann, *Latomus* XII (1953) 53-69.

possession of a genuine talent for poetry he was sharply distinguished from his putative associates, I would still expect, before accepting Brakman's proposal, to find some signs of sympathy with the literary, as well as religious, values of fashionable paganism. It is the lack of any such indication which convinces me that the author of the *Pervigilium* should not be sought in the smart literary salons of fourth-century Rome.

So far, beyond the qualified acceptance of A.D. 350 as a *terminus post quem* for the composition of the *Pervigilium*, my argument has been largely negative. Is it possible to reach any more positive conclusions about the authorship of this fascinating poem ? The search to identify the poet with some known figure has proved fruitless, and I have no new names to canvass, but I would like to lend my support to the cautious proposal of Boyancé : that the *Pervigilium* may be the work of a poetess ([18]).

Boyancé points out that historical *pervigilia* were associated particularly with women ([19]), and that the only named worshippers in our *pervigilium* are virgin nymphs. If the vigil culminates in a festival of initiation, as I believe, then we must certainly assume a male presence, but Boyancé is still right to insist that the maiden's longing for marriage is an important motif. He also draws some largely chimerical comparisons between the *Pervigilium* and the poetry of Sappho.

Fortunately we can support this conjecture by more substantial considerations, for as early as line 3 the verb *nubunt* indicates that the poet is thinking of birds as brides, while in the following line the *nemus* is personified as a woman loosening her hair to the caress of the showers. In stanza III the traditional symbolism of the rose, a warning to women to employ their fleeting charms, an invitation to men to enjoy woman's beauty before it fades, is transformed into a metaphor for the stirring desire of a young maiden. This feminine emphasis is preserved, in the stanzas describing the festival itself, by the central rôle of the chorus of virgins.

The eighth stanza glorifies Venus as the divine *genetrix* of the Roman people. Line seventy refers to the marriage of Aeneas and Lavinia :

>   *ipsa Laurentem puellam coniugem nato dedit.*

---

(18) Boyancé, *REL* XXVIII (1950), 212-35 ; *id.* (1966), 1560-3, where he suggests Julia Balbilla, a contemporary of Hadrian, as the possible poetess of the *P.V.*
(19) Boyancé (1950), 218.

Our attention is focused, not upon Venus' son, but upon the girl Lavinia and her destiny as *coniunx*. Similarly when the poet alludes to the rape of Rhea Silvia, the reader's gaze is directed, not towards Mars, but to Rhea herself and her earlier status as *pudica virgo*.

But most interesting of all are lines 86-90, where the poet longs to share the universal experience of spring. In spring the virgin roses unfold in answer to love's summons, in spring Venus initiates the virgin nymphs into the sacraments of love. The *P.V.*, it is true, does not deal exclusively with female initiation but it represents a predominant emphasis and, when the poet prays for a personal spring, this surely expresses a desire to share the awakening of rose and nymph. And what is it that immediately precedes, and even provokes, the poet's anxious self-questioning ? It is the song of *Terei puella* and of her *soror*, of the wife and her sister. The silent poet longs to join the swallow, the sister, and to transmute silence into song. Now it is quite possible that a man might compare his silent grief with the song of the nightingale or the swallow [20], but I think it strange that he should at the same time *insist* upon their mythological significance as wife and sister. This emphasis, in a context so intimately bound up with the deepest longings of the poet, betokens, together with those passages discussed above, the feelings and imaginative response of a woman.

I am led to conclude that the *Pervigilium* is probably the work of a fourth century poetess, possibly an African, but, knowing of no suitable figure with whom to identify her, commend this research to the patient industry of scholars more knowledgeable than myself [21].

---

(20) Cf. Catullus LXV, 11-14, for example.

(21) My theory about the sex of our poet is offered with due circumspection. I apply masculine pronouns and adjectives to the author throughout this study. Those convinced by my arguments here will experience no difficulty in making the appropriate substitutions.

The Festival

In their interpretation of the festival which is evoked with such impressionistic power in the *Pervigilium Veneris* scholars have again, as with the question of date, split into two broad parties : those who, with Mackail, regard both the poem and the festival as a 'motive of fantasy, a summons which evokes imaginative associations and sets the rhythm of poetry in movement round nature and history, love and life' [1], and those who believe that the *Pervigilium* was inspired by, if not specifically written for, a local Sicilian festival belonging to the ritual of one of the ancient townships called Hybla [2]. I will explain below why I am convinced that the *Pervigilium* is not a genuinely liturgical poem [3] and why I believe that the Hyblaean setting should not be interpreted literally, but neither of these negative considerations precludes the possibility that the ritual of the *Pervigilium* reflects genuine features of Roman worship. This chapter is thus a search for possible sources of the poet's religious impressionism.

That the festival is a spring-celebration in honour of the birth of Venus is beyond doubt, for the second stanza unambiguously proclaims why the 'tomorrow' of the poem is so sacred a day. Cazzaniga's attempt to explain

---

(1) MACKAIL (1912), 345, quoted with approval by CLEMENTI 73-4. But both Mackail and Clementi qualify their interpretation of the festival as a creation of fancy by arguing that it was suggested to the poet by the ritual of the *Festum Veneris et Virilis Fortunae*, celebrated in Rome at the beginning of April and described by OVID (*Fast*. IV, 133-162). This is unlikely, since Ovid's festival is attended by sexually-experienced women and is primarily a festival of purification, whereas the *P.V.* is a ceremony of initiation. Schilling also believes that our festival is an imaginative creation, but one written 'en marge des cérémonies officielles' in the time of Hadrian.

(2) Notably CAZZANIGA, 47-63. LATKOCZY (1894) argued that the *P.V.* was written for a Hyblaean festival celebrated in 123 during Hadrian's visit to Sicily. BOYANCÉ (1966), 1560-2, modifies Latkoczy's proposal : the setting of the *P.V.* in Hybla reflects Hadrian's interest in Sicily ; the poem is the work of a court poet projecting the enthusiasms of the Emperor. Hyblaean ritual is presented as a model for Hadrian's planned innovations in Rome itself. For the true significance of Hybla, cf. pp. 30-33.

(3) Cf. the last paragraph of this chapter.

the festival as a commemoration of the *hieros gamos* of Venus and Anchises is based on almost wilful misinterpretation of stanza three and utterly lacks conviction [4]. The *Pervigilium* celebrates the birthday of Venus. In this context Boyancé [5] has drawn our attention to the witness of three mosaics, and to an illustrated calendar of A.D. 354, which depict figures dancing round a statue of Ἀφροδίτη ἀναδυομένη. The appropriate illustration in the calendar is for the *Veneralia* of April the first, while one of the mosaics is a tableau of the months with the relevant scene belonging to April, probably to the Kalends of that month. Particularly interesting in the light of this evidence is line 7 of the *Pervigilium* :

>   *cras Dione iura dicit fulta sublimi throno,*

for in the calendar and mosaics the figure of Venus is raised upon a column. Is it this which the poetic imagination has transformed into the presence of the goddess herself throned in splendour ? In the mosaic of Thysdrus, moreover, the worshippers carry torches, a detail which suggests the night-revelry described in lines 42-7 of the *Pervigilium* [6], which seems, therefore, at least in its broadest outline, to represent an imaginative recreation of a real feature of Roman religious life : the celebration in April of the birthday of Ἀφροδίτη ἀναδυομένη. The *Pervigilium* is virtually the only literary witness to the existence of such a festival [7], and there is no evidence to suggest that the birthday of Venus ever constituted an important part of formal state-religion in Rome itself. The mosaics from Carthage, Thysdrus and Ostia suggest a tradition which flourished independently in different localities ; the birthday of Venus was

---

(4) CAZZANIGA, 63-75 ; cf. my notes to line 23 for the rejection of his arguments.

(5) BOYANCÉ (1966), 1547-52.

(6) BOYANCÉ (1966), 1548-9.

(7) DRACONTIUS, *Romul.* VIII, 435-9, is the only other passage I know in which a Roman writer mentions a festival in honour of Venus' birth :

>   *Cypro festa dies natalis forte Dionae*
>   *illa luce fuit ; veniunt ad sacra Cytherae*
>   *reddere vota deae quidquid capit insula Cypros,*
>   *quod nemus Idalium, quod continet alta Cythera,*
>   *quod Paphon exornat, tacitas quod lustrat Amyclas.*

This is from a poem *de raptu Helenae* and its festival takes place in Cyprus ; the passage, therefore, is certainly not conclusive evidence for the celebration, in Dracontius' time, of Venus' *dies natalis*, but he is unlikely, even in a mythological context, to have introduced a festival which never existed ; he must have been familiar, either from life or literature, with rituals commemorating the birth of Venus.

perhaps a local festival common to many communities in the Roman
world, rather than a central feature of imperial religion. There seems, at
least, to be little justification for associating the *Pervigilium*, and the ritual
there described, with the religious innovations of the Emperor Hadrian or
any of his successors.

The festival is in honour of Ἀφροδίτη ἀναδυομένη ; so much is certain.
Less obvious is the nature of the ceremony which formed the central
feature of this festival. Here our attention must focus upon stanzas 4-6 and
the part played by the nymphs in the ritual of the *Pervigilium*. Boyancé is
right to insist upon the importance of the nuptial motif but is vague about
the precise role of the virgin nymphs [8]. Are they attendants of the
goddess ? Is their innocence to be preserved ? Cazzaniga [9] argues that
they are the consecrated virgins of the grove of Hyblaean Venus and
specifically denies that they will surrender their virginity at any stage of
the festival. But why should we exclude this possibility ? Remember the
refrain, which is a universal summons to love, a summons to virgins as
well as the sexually experienced, remember stanza III where the
unfolding of the rose symbolises the awakening desire of the maiden, a
desire which is to culminate in sexual dedication, remember stanza V
where Diana is excluded from the festival because it is unbecoming for a
virgin to attend. Can we doubt against such evidence that the nymphs of
the central stanzas will sacrifice their innocence upon the altar of love, or
that this surrender is the central feature of their worship ?

In thus presenting the *Pervigilium* as a festival of initiation the poet
concentrates upon the first half of the refrain. The *myrteae casae*,
specially made by Venus as *copulatrix amorum*, are clearly the bowers of
love where this initiation is to be experienced. Now in Ovid's description
of the feast of Anna Perenna [10] the *frondea casa* performs a similar
function :

> plebs venit ac virides passim disiecta per herbas
>   potat, et accumbit cum pare quisque sua.
> sub Iove pars durat, pauci tentoria ponunt,
>   sunt quibus e ramis frondea facta casa est.   (*Fast*. III, 525-8)

Martial also states (IV, 64, 16-17) that the sanctuary of Anna Perenna
'delights in virgin's blood'. Explaining Martial's allusion to *cruore virgineo*

---

(8) BOYANCÉ (1950), 212-35.
(9) CAZZANIGA, 76.
(10) Cf. Schilling's discussion of the passage, XXXVIII-IX.

with reference to the drunken licence of Ovid's festival, Sir James Fraser almost bashfully concluded, 'it was a day of Valentines, and into the tents and huts on the greensward of the grove many a girl may have gone in a maid who came out a maid no more' [11]. There can be no doubt that the virgins of the *Pervigilium* will encounter a similar fate in the myrtle bowers of the 'love-binder'.

But the poet of the *Pervigilium* has not necessarily lifted his huts straight from the ritual of another goddess and appropriately made them of myrtle. The Ἔρωτες of pseudo-Lucian contains a description of a temple to Aphrodite on Cnidos [12], a temple surrounded by a grove of myrtles, cypresses, plane-trees and laurels. The trees are covered with amorous ivy and grape-laden vines ; τερπνοτέρα γὰρ Ἀφροδίτη μετὰ Διονύσου (cf. *P.V.* line 45). The description continues : ἦν δε ὑπὸ ταῖς ἄγαν παλινσκίοις ὕλαις ἱλαραὶ κλισίαι τοῖς ἐνεστιᾶσθαι θέλουσιν, εἰς ἃ τῶν μὲν ἀστικῶν σπανίως ἐπεφοίτων τινές, ἀθρόος δ' ὁ πολιτικὸς ὄχλος ἐπανηγύριζεν ὄντως ἀφροδισιάζοντες. Here again, and this time in the sanctuary of Venus herself, are *casae* (for κλίσιαι are their Greek equivalent) in which lovers lie.

The bowers of the *Pervigilium* thus seem to have been a genuine feature of pagan religion, bowers in which the devotees of Anna Perenna lay in drunken embrace, bowers where the people of Cnidos concealed and by the same token demonstrated their subservience to the goddess of love.

The sexual freedom which both Ovid and Lucian mention appears to have belonged to the indulgence of a pagan festival as the consummation of a drunken debauch. But Augustine and Valerius Maximus describe ceremonies involving the submission of virgins to intercourse with strangers as a ritual of central importance ; this is the sacramental initiation of virgins, performed in temples of Venus as a prelude to marriage and as an expression of reverence for the goddess [13]. Both writers are discussing contemporary African practice, while Strabo and Lucian mention similar customs on Cyprus and Biblos [14]. These rituals seem to have been regarded with some embarrassment by out ancient authorities (or with gloomy relish, in the case of the Christian polemecists, as yet another instance of pagan debauchery) ; they are certainly of eastern

---

(11) *The Fasti of Ovid* (London, 1929), vol. III, 113 (on *Fast.* III, 523).
(12) This description, and the quotations below, are from Ἔρωτες 12.
(13) AUG., *De Civ. Dei* IV, 10 ; VAL. MAX. 2, 6, 15.
(14) STRAB., 272 ; LUC., *De Dea Syria*, 6.

origin, as was Aphrodite, and, unlike Aphrodite, probably gained no more than a foothold in Graeco-Roman religion. And yet the solemn defloration of virgins, as a ritual of worship, lies at the heart of the *Pervigilium*. It is at least possible that sacral initiation before marriage, in which the virgin vowed the first-fruits of experience to the goddess, was a feature of the religion of love familiar to our poet through literature or through more direct acquaintance with a cult-tradition. The literary medium is far more likely to have been the channel of influence, since such rites were not of wide distribution and could not have constituted a generally acknowledged feature of the cult of Ἀφροδίτη ἀναδυομένη without having attracted more attention to themselves. Moreover the central ceremony of the *Pervigilium* is not a ritual of premarital initiation, it is the initiation of marriage itself. The trembling virgin, exposed to a stranger's lust, has become a blushing bride ; sacral prostitution has been transformed into marital dedication ; maidens have turned into nymphs and ritual has been translated into fantasy. We are not, apparently, dealing with a poetic version of a local rite of initiation, a version which consciously distorts the rituals it describes, but with a shadowy background of ideas and observances which may have influenced the poet in his creation of the vigil of Venus. If the fundamental nature of the festival was suggested to the poet, however indirectly, by the strange rites mentioned above, then the poetic imagination has metamorphosised the influences working upon it. The festival, which is no less than a service of mass initiation and matrimony, is surely an imaginative creation, but not a fantasy of pure invention ; different strands of ritual and religion are woven together to form an impressionistic tapestry, which is important, not as an account of a local festival, but as the externalisation and expression of the poet's own longing for experience of love.

Previous editors have rightly maintained that the poet avoids any suggestion of the genial licence described by Ovid with such evident affection in his account of the feast of Anna Perenna ([15]). They also point out that in Roman literature the word *pervigilium* is virtually synonymous with riot and debauchery ([16]), emphasising that there is no hint of either in the *Pervigilium Veneris*. And yet they do not insist, as I have done, that the festival is to culminate in sexual experience. Propriety is preserved by the introduction of the nuptial-motif, a feature which I have already

---

(15) Notably SCHILLING, cf. references in note 10.
(16) CLEMENTI, 72-3.

emphasised. The notion of marriage is explicit as early as line 3, and is mentioned again in lines 22, 59 and 72, whereas the whole of stanza III is a metaphor evoking the virgin's response to the promptings of love, an emotional metamorphosis which is to find fulfilment in marriage and sexual union. In this way the conceptual background of the poem conditions our reaction to the ritual of the festival, which is thought of as matrimonial dedication rather than sexual indulgence. The poet's emphasis, too, is upon emotional, rather than physical, experience, and the real nature of the festival, although obvious, is grasped by inference and is nowhere baldly stated.

The setting of the festival is the sacred grove, the *lucus myrteus* of the goddess, but by an imaginative extension the devotees of love invade and annex the glades (*saltus tuos*) of the virgin huntress, and Diana's territory becomes part of the domain of the Queen of Love. The formal procession to the grove (stanza IV), the threatening presence of Cupid, and Diana's exile, might derive either from local ritual or from literature. Ceres, Bacchus and Apollo, as the essential sponsors of any festive occasion, are equally at home in either tradition.

The virgins who are to answer the summons of love are no ordinary virgins. They are the nymphs of the surrounding countryside. Indeed the whole festival is removed beyond common reality into a Sicilian fairyland where the living gods walk upon the earth. The references to Hybla (49-52) are, in my opinion, intended to enhance the magical atmosphere of the poem, although they have normally been interpreted as setting the *Pervigilium* in a precise, geographical location.

Of the three ancient Sicilian townships called Hybla, Clementi, Schilling and Cazzaniga all agree that Hybla Gereatis is the Hybla of the *Pervigilium* ([17]), not only because it lay on the slopes of Aetna (cf. 52), but because Pausanias (V, 23, 6) mentions that it contained a 'sanctuary of the Hyblaean goddess honoured by the Sicilians', and because an inscription (*C.I.L.* X, 7013) survives bearing the dedication *Veneri victrici Hyblensi*. Hybla Gereatis' situation, its reputation as a religious centre, and the probable identification of Pausanias' Hyblaean goddess with *Venus Victrix*, all make it a tempting proposition as the home of the *Pervigilium Veneris*. I will explain below why I regard this evidence with extreme

(17) Clementi and Schilling, notes to 49 ; for Cazzaniga's argument cf. references in following note.

suspicion, but would like firstly to consider Cazzaniga's argument that the
Pervigilium represents the literary refinement of Sicilian, more precisely
of Hyblaean, ritual [18].

As a prelude several towns in Sicily are associated with the legend of
Uranus' castration, after which, with specific concern for Hybla Gereatis,
Cazzaniga draws our attention to the following entry in Nonius Marcellus
(CXVIII, 27) : *gerrae : nugae, ineptiae ; et sunt gerrae fascini* [19] *qui sic in
Naxo, insula Veneris, ab incolis appellantur*. From this Cazzaniga derives
the epithet 'gereatis', thus associating Hybla Gereatis with a cult of sexual
potency in which the *fascinus*, symbolising both the male and female
genital organs, was a ritual object. But even if this etymology is correct
and Hybla was the centre of such a cult, the *Pervigilium* itself contains no
traces of phallic ritual or imagery [20]. The poet, on the assumption that his
festival has its roots in Hyblaean phallism, has so drastically reshaped his
material that it no longer betrays any traces of its origins.

Cazzaniga further points to a passage in Athenaeus (250 a) which
describes a Sicilian vigil :

> ... ἔθους ὄντος κατὰ Σικελίαν θυσίας ποιεῖσθαι κατὰ τὰς οἰκίας ταῖς
> Νύμφαις καὶ περὶ τὰ ἀγάλματα παννυχίζειν μεθυσκομένους ὀρχεῖσθαί τε περὶ τὰς
> θεάς .

The nymphs here mentioned are identified with those of the *Pervigilium*
who represent, according to Cazzaniga, the ever-virgin attendants of
the grove of Hyblaean Venus. But Athenaeus is here discussing an
observance of the fourth century B.C., he mentions neither Aphrodite nor
Hybla, and his vigil is a drunken revel in honour of the nymphs, whereas
the nymphs of the *P.V.* are themselves devotees and not objects of
worship. This passage of Athenaeus has nothing to tell us about either
Hybla or the *Pervigilium Veneris*.

In a postscript to his *Saggio critico* Cazzaniga reexamines the
significance of a Sicilian coin with the inscription ῞ΥΒΛΑΣ ΜΕΓΑ-
ΛᾹΣ [21], a stamp which has formally been taken as proclaiming the coin's

---

(18) CAZZANIGA, 46-63, 63-78.
(19) The word *fascinus* normally refers to the male genitals only, but it is here a
synonym for *gerrae*, for the meaning of which Cazzaniga further cites *Paroem Graec*.
app. I, 72 (Leutsch-Scheid.) : Γέρρα Νάξια : γέρρα Σικελιοὶ λέγουσι τὰ ἀνδρεῖα καὶ γυναχεῖα
αἰδοῖα. ἦν δὲ ἐν τῇ Σικελιχῇ Νάξῳ τέμενος ἐπιθαλάσσιον Ἀφροδίτης ἐν ᾧ μεγάλα αἰδοῖα
ἀνέχειτο.
(20) Except possibly for the phrase *rigentibus floribus* in line 58.
(21) CAZZANIGA, 'Una moneta di Hybla ed il v. 45 del *P.V.*', *SCO* III (1955), 134-40.

town of origin, Ὕβλα μείζων rather than Hybla Gereatis. But Cazzaniga argues that this inscription is not a genitive of origin, but one of dedication : to the great goddess of Hybla Gereatis. He then identifies the female head on the coin's obverse with Hybla-Ceres, the figure on the reverse with Dionysus, and explains line 45 of the *Pervigilium* as a reference to Hyblaean ritual.

This whole train of thought is misconceived. Can we be sure that the name of the Hyblaean goddess was identical with that of the town where she was worshipped ? Can we safely identify this goddess with Ceres as well as with Venus, or confidently assume that the figure on the reverse of the coin is Dionysus (Head [22] *ad loc.* is doubtful about this) ? Moreover the numismatic analogies which Cazzaniga cites in support of his argument only confound the theory they are supposed to confirm ; for all the coins mentioned (Head 100, 123, 125, 154-6), stamped with the name of a tutelary god, bear the inscription of dedication on the obverse together with the figure, while the inscription of our coin is on the reverse with the head of the goddess on the obverse. The legend YBΛAS MEΓAΛAS must, as has generally been assumed, refer to the town where the coin was minted and cannot be used to reconstruct the rites of Hybla Gereatis. There is no reason to assume that the presence of Ceres or Bacchus reflects a specifically Hyblaean practice ; they appear in their universally acknowledged status as patrons of growth, plenty and good cheer.

The search for local tradition beneath the surface of the *Pervigilium* has been unsuccessful. There remains the poet's repeated mention of Hybla in lines 49-52 :

> iussit Hyblaeis tribunal stare diva floribus ;
> praeses ipsa iura dicit, adsederunt Gratiae ;
> Hybla totos funde flores, quidquid annus adtulit !
> Hybla florum sume vestem, quantus Aetnae campus est !

It is perhaps significant that the references to Hybla occur more than half way through the poem in a context where the poet is developing a metaphor drawn from legal, not religious, procedure, a metaphor which suggests the free play of the imagination rather than the faithful description of a local tradition of worship. But even more important is the manner of Hybla's introduction : *Hyblaeis floribus, totos flores, florum*

(22) HEAD, B. V., *Historia Numorum* (Oxford 1911), 147-8.

vestem. It is quite clear that to the poet Hybla means flowers; this association is, in my opinion, far more likely to explain the setting of the *Pervigilium* than the existence of a cult of Hyblaean Venus.

In Virgil we hear bees from Hybla buzzing in the Italian landscape of the first *Eclogue* (53) and the sweetness of Hyblaean thyme is obviously proverbial (*Ecl.* VII, 37). Martial turns to Hybla as the supreme example of a fertile landscape (II, 46, 1-2), while in Claudian's day Hybla's fame is still undiminished (cf. *De Rapt. Pros.* II, 79-80), and its reputation even survives into the Middle Ages (cf. *Carm. Bur.* 119, 13). The treatment of Hybla in the *Pervigilium*, therefore, where the poet exploits its reputation as a place famous for its flowers, persuades me that it is this tradition which explains the Hyblaean setting of Venus' court of love. Our poet may have been Sicilian and a cult of Hyblaean Venus may have flourished in Sicily, but the introduction of Hybla is probably not intended to place the festival in a particular centre of Venus' worship. Rather it sets the *Pervigilium* amongst the fabled glades of a proverbially rich landscape.

The festival then celebrates the birth of Venus. Its climax will be the initiation of the nymphs into the sexual mysteries of the goddess, a ceremony which will take place in the *myrteae casae* which adorn Venus' sanctuary. The occasion of the *Pervigilium*, also the *casae* and their function, seem to have been suggested by existing features of Roman religion but, although sexual indulgence clearly formed a constituent of some aspects of ancient worship, it is highly unlikely that a service of mass sexual-initiation ever occupied a central position in the ritual of Ἀφροδίτη ἀναδυομένη. The core of the *Pervigilium* is therefore a product of the imagination, a projection of the sexual yearnings of the poet, and not an accurate reflection of genuine ritual, Hyblaean or otherwise.

The evocation of the festival is enriched by the nuptial-motif, which forms a framework for the ceremonies of the central stanzas and preserves the decorum of what might otherwise seem a promiscuous revel. The procession of stanza IV, Diana's exile in stanza V, the presence of Ceres, Bacchus and Apollo in line 45, might derive from either a religious or a literary tradition, but, whatever the origin of the various rituals of the *Pervigilium*, they are transported into a world beyond reality where gods and demi-gods mingle in a Sicilian paradise.

If my conclusions about the festival are correct, then it follows that the *Pervigilium* cannot be a liturgical composition in the sense of Horace's *Carmen Saeculare*, and the closing lines of the poem, which are dominated by the presence of the poet himself, have generally been held to preclude the possibility that it could have been written for any official purpose. But the form of the *Pervigilium* is that of a festival hymn, and Boyancé has suggested that the whole poem, with the exception of the last five lines, should be interpreted as the solemn chant of the choir of virgins, that the poet himself does not speak until line 89 [23]. This is most unlikely. Note how both Catullus and Horace, when writing poetry in the genre of choral celebration, make this fact quite obvious from the start. I cannot believe that our poet, who refers to the nymphs in the third person throughout stanzas IV and VI, would expect us to infer from *rogamus* alone (in line 38) that the poem is to be placed on the lips of the *virgines-nymphae*, and that he would then conclude with an unannounced modulation into personal speech. Far more probable is that the fifth stanza is introduced as a choral interlude to enhance the festival atmosphere of the poem, and that elsewhere the poet speaks *in propria persona* : both his words of praise and worship, as he surveys the activity of the goddess in the world at large, and his prayer for help, when he almost stumbles upon the barren silence in his own heart.

(23) BOYANCÉ (1950), 217ff.

The Metre

The *Pervigilium Veneris* is written in trochaic tetrameters catalectic [1]. The poet's general practice is clear enough and conforms with the usage of Greek poets and their stricter Roman followers. Spondaic, anapaestic and dactylic feet, though permitted in the second unit of each metron, are excluded from its first foot which is a pure trochee unless resolved into a tribrach. There is only one instance of such resolution in the *Pervigilium* (*posuit* line 31) and our poet is more reluctant than most other Roman poets to admit anapaestic resolution into the last foot of the metron.

But the metrical pattern outlined above is violated by the MSS in the following cases :

     35 : spondee in 3rd foot (*in armis*)
     50 : spondees in 1st and 5th feet (*praesens, adsederunt*)
60, 91 : spondees in fifth foot (*vernis, nec me*)
55, 62 : anapaests in fifth foot (*Pueri, aleret*)

These instances all disregard the rule governing the first foot of the metron, a rule observed elsewhere in the poem and by other writers of strict tetrameters. An editor must decide whether, given the general pattern of the *P.V.*, each such usage is merely unorthodox or metrically impossible. Is the assumption of conformity to a Greek standard of metre a valid criterion for emendation or rearrangement, as Clementi and others have believed [2], or should we agree with Rand [3] that : 'It is dangerous to claim for a poet a perfect metrical standard and then to emend away his exceptions in order that his standard may be perfect' ? What precedents or analogies, if any, exist elsewhere in Roman tetrameters for occasional departures from a metrical norm ?

---

(1) For a good introduction to the metre and its relative the trochaic septenarius cf. D. S. RAVEN, *Latin Metre* (London, 1965), 74-83.

(2) Clementi keeps the fifth-foot anapaests, but gets rid of fifth-foot spondees, through adopting humanist conjectures, and accepts Saumaise's rearrangement of 35. Amongst more recent editors to do the same have been Owen and Mackail.

(3) RAND (1934), 8.

Republican verse

The trochaic septenarius, a very close relative of the tetrameter, is a common metre in Roman comedy and also appears in extant fragments of Varro, Lucilius and Porcius Licinus [4]. The scattered remains of republican lampoons and marching songs [5] show that the metre was also a favourite in popular, as well as more serious, verse. Spondees are freely admitted into all but the seventh foot and are very common in the first half of the metron. Resolution is used with such frequency throughout the line that identification of the metre is sometimes difficult.

Brakman and Schilling [6] both appeal to the septenarius as a justification of the metrical peculiarities of the *P.V.*, but, if our poet had followed the example of Plautus and Terence, then spondaic and anapaestic feet in the first foot of the metron would be a continual feature of his verse, not an occasional licence, if genuine. The *Pervigilium*, in which the modification of Greek usage is very moderate, clearly belongs to a different metrical tradition than the trochaic septenarius. Schilling is therefore wrong, in his thoroughly inadequate discussion of the metre, to claim that the *P.V.* represents a return to a republican verse tradition. The septenarius cannot be adduced as a precedent for the metrical practice of our poet.

Seneca and Florus

Neglected by the poets of the golden age, the trochaic tetrameter makes three brief appearances in Senecan tragedy [7]. These passages are modelled on Greek usage and are metrically flawless, as one would expect. Seneca is also, in accordance with Greek practice, notably freer in his admission of resolution than is the poet of the *Pervigilium*.

If the attribution of the codex Salmasianus can be trusted, then the poet Florus (*flor.* 125 A.D.) wrote a group of short poems in tetrameters collectively entitled *De Qualitate Vitae* [8]. The metre is fairly strict, with the exception of one remarkable line :

(4) For Varro, cf. *Satires Ménippées*, ed. J. P. Cèbe (Paris, 1972-5) III vols. ; vol. I, 30 ; vol. II, 198, 201-2 ; vol. III, 326. For Licinus cf. Morel, *Frag. Poet. Lat.*, 44-5.
(5) For popular septenarii cf. Morel 92, 30, 42, 133.
(6) Brakman (1928), 67-8 ; Schilling, XV-XVI.
(7) *Med.* 740-51 ; *Oed.* 223-32 ; *Phaedr.* 1201-12.
(8) *A.L.* 245-52 ; the *cod. Thuaneus* attributes the verses to a certain Floridus.

> *omnis mulier intra pectus celat virus pestilens*   (246, 1)

This solitary septenarius, with spondees in the first, third and fifth feet, might be a popular verse incorporated into the poem as a general statement of the theme briefly developed in the next line. But more likely is that the word order has been disrupted and should be restored as follows [9] :

> *mulier intra pectus omnis celat virus pestilens.*

This reduces the irregularity to a fifth-foot spondee, which is inescapable and seems to be confirmed as a usage of the poet by the following line where the text is not seriously in doubt :

> *ambo de donis calorem, vite et radio, conferunt.*   (247, 3)

TIBERIANUS

The fifth-foot spondee is also a feature of Tiberianus' tetrameters, for in his *Amnis ibat* [10] the rule governing the fifth-foot is violated in line 6 :

> *et croco solum rubebat et lucebat liliis,*

and again in line 14 :

> *qua fluenta labibunda guttis ibant lucidis.*

EARLY CHRISTIAN HYMNS

The tetrameters of Hilary of Poitiers [11] are metrically crude ; bristling with false quantities and with spondees admitted at random, they obviously belong to a popular, not a literary, tradition. By contrast the tetrameters of Prudentius and the much later Fortunatus are surprisingly rigorous [12]. Indeed in Fortunatus' magnificent *Pange lingua*, although the shortening of metrically long syllables is frequent, the metrical *form* of the verse is flawless. Prudentius is not beyond a false quantity [13], but his

---

(9) This rearrangement appears without comment in Wight DUFF, *Minor Latin Poets* (London, 1934), 426 ; BAEHRENS, *PLM* IV, 347 assigns it to Piersonus.

(10) Text in BAEHRENS, *PLM* III, 263.

(11) Text in W. BULST, *Hymni Lat. Antiquissimi LXXV, Psalmi* III (Heidelberg, 1956), 34-5.

(12) PRUDENTIUS, *Cath.* I & X ; FORT. II, 2 (LEO, *M.G.H.*).

(13) *Cath.* I, 3, where the short 2nd syllable of *eadem* (nom. neut. plural) must be read as a long syllable (if the text is correct).

only departure from structural orthodoxy is the presence of a fifth-foot spondee in *Cath.* X, 40 :

> *extimum vestis sacratae furtim mulier attigit.*

We also possess very short tetrameter poems by pseudo-Ausonius, by Luxorius and by Fulgentius. The tetrameters of ps.-Ausonius contain a third-foot spondee [14], those of Luxorius are strict [15], while Fulgentius' use of the metre betrays widespread ignorance of simple prosody and is not relevant to the present investigation [16].

The emendation of spondaic fifth-feet in the text of the *Pervigilium* is based on a strict application of Greek metrical rules to Roman practice. But the evidence of the Roman poets themselves, of Florus, of Tiberianus, of Prudentius and, most notably, of our own poet, suggests that they modified Greek rigidity by allowing an occasional spondee in the fifth foot, while at the same time preserving the trochaic impulse of the metre by rejecting the spondaic licence of the Roman septenarius. *Adsederunt* (50), *vernis* (60) and *nec me* (91) are retained with confidence. It is not as easy to find parallels for the anapaestic fifth feet in 55 and 62 but the argument from metrical purity is clearly unconvincing and no other considerations suggest that alteration is required.

The spondaic first foot in line 50 is a different matter. This is the only instance of such a usage in the *Pervigilium*, we have encountered no analogies in tetrameters of a similar type, and Scaliger's *praeses* is a simple correction perfectly suited to its context. Sense, the poet's metrical practice, and the metrical tradition to which the *P.V.* belongs, all, therefore, expose the corruption of the MSS reading *praesens*.

The case of the third-foot spondee in 35 is more complex. This spondee is the result of an emendation which is so simple and convincing that it demands acceptance, but the only analogy for such a usage is a line of ps.-Ausonius where the text is uncertain. The MSS word-order is retained, but with caution. Salmasius' rearrangement may be right :

> *est in armis totus idem quando nudus est Amor.*

---

(14) Cf. Aus. XXII.I, 5, 2 :

> *par pari iugator coniunx ; quidquid inpar dissidet.*

(15) *A.L.* 291.

(16) But cf. concluding paragraph of the chapter, and FULG., *Mythologia* (ed. Helm, 1898), pp. 7-8.

Discussion has so far been aimed at the text, but the poet's metrical habits might also provide some clues concerning the date and authorship of the *Pervigilium*, although the occasional features, which our argument has previously concentrated upon, provide no such indication in themselves, being equally at home in the age of Florus (second century) and the age of Tiberianus (fourth).

Both these poets have been proposed by previous scholars as the author of the *Pervigilium*. I have disposed of Florus' candidature elsewhere ([17]) in this study, but worthy of comment in the present context is that his tetrameters are distinguished from those of the *Pervigilium* by several significant metrical considerations. Florus is free in his use of elision which, with the exception of the refrain, is employed very sparingly in the *P.V.* Again quadrisyllables at the line-ending, while obviously quite acceptable to Florus who uses them three times in twenty six lines, were clearly less pleasing to the poet of the *Pervigilium* who employs only one such usage (in the penultimate line of the poem). Florus is also notably fonder of resolution, a technique employed with moderation in the *Pervigilium*, and, in particular, Florus freely admits tribrachs, which are all but excluded from the *P.V.* (only at line 31). Florus' use of trochaic tetrameters therefore emerges, when analysed, as an argument against, not in favour of, his authorship of the *Pervigilium*.

Our poet's aversion for quadrisyllabes at the end of lines is shared by Tiberianus in his *Amnis ibat*, where none of the poem's twenty lines concludes with a quadrisyllable. This fact was noticed by Fort who explained the avoidance of quadrisyllabic words in this position as a technique of harmonising the accent of stress and the beat of metrical ictus ([18]). This is certainly true of Tiberianus, who only twice employs disyllabes at the line-ending. Eighteen out of twenty lines thus end with trisyllables and coincidence between accent and ictus. It is obviously in pursuit of such agreement that Tiberianus has outlawed quadrisyllables and severely restricted his admission of disyllabic words to conclude his lines. But the poet of the *Pervigilium* frequently ends his tetrameters with disyllables and the generally resulting clash between the beat of the rhythm and stress of pronunciation. Widespread coincidence of accent and ictus is a conspicuous feature of the *Amnis ibat throughout the line*, but not, as has been wrongly claimed by Fort and others, of the *Pervigi-*

(17) Cf. 'Date and Authorship', p. 21-22.
(18) J. A. Fort, 'The *Pervigilium Veneris* in quatrains', (Oxford, 1922) *appendix*.

lium Veneris ; for there conflict is very frequent both at the beginning (i.e.
2nd foot) and end of the line, and occurs in every foot but the fourth (and,
of course the first). Our poet's practice in this matter, in spite of the
differences noted above, is far nearer that of Florus than of Tiberianus.
Why he has virtually excluded quadrisyllables at the end of the line is less
obvious than with Tiberianus, but Fort is mistaken in regarding distaste
for such endings as an aversion exclusive to the *Pervigilium* and the *Amnis
ibat*, for a four-syllable word occurs only once, and this a Graecism, at the
line-ending in Seneca's tetrameters [19]. He finishes almost every line with
a disyllable. Perhaps both Seneca and the poet of the *Pervigilium* felt that
caesura in the sixth foot, followed by a single word to conclude the line,
produced an exaggerated and unpleasant break in the flow of the
tetrameter. Certainly, with their ready admission of disyllables in this
position, neither poet was guided by the search for accentual and
rhythmical harmony.

The avoidance of quadrisyllabic words to end the line in both the
Pervigilium and the *Amnis ibat* is not governed by a common purpose,
and coincidence of accent and ictus is a far more marked feature of the
Amnis ibat than of the *Pervigilium*. A further significant contrast is that
the *Pervigilium* contains no purely trochaic line, while there are three
certain such instances in the twenty lines of the *Amnis ibat*. Furthermore
whenever, in the *Pervigilium*, the first half of the line contains no real
caesura, consisting of disyllables separated by diaeresis between the feet,
the flow of the line, and the danger of metrical monotony, is always
checked by spondees in the last foot of each metron. The one exception is
line 50 :

> *praeses ipsa iura dicit, adsederunt Gratiae,*

where the threat of disintegration into a rhythmical jingle is emphatically
halted by the four spondaic syllables of *adsederunt*. We meet no line like :

> *amnis ibat inter arva valle fusus frigida.*

Here the trochaic disyllables, the absence of true caesura, and the
complete correspondence of accentual stress and rythmical ictus,
establishes a tempo which is a less obvious but marked tendency of the
poem as a whole, a tempo which effectively communicates the vitality of

(19) *Med.* 745.

the scene the poet is describing, but which would become tedious in a poem much longer than the *Amnis ibat*.

The poet of the *Pervigilium* is far freer in his use of spondees, while at the same time he preserves the trochaic impetus of his verse ; together with the sparing admission of resolution and the ever-present tension between passages where accent and ictus coincide, and passages where these principles of stress are in conflict, this creates an effect of suppressed urgency, of weight as well as speed, of constant rhythmical variety which represents a metrical achievement of an altogether higher order than that of the *Amnis ibat*.

With regard to the authorship of the *Pervigilium* the metrical argument is a negative one, pointing neither to Florus, Tiberianus or any other known user of tetrameters. As to the question of date, the metre indicates what we know already : that the poem belongs somewhere in the post-classical period, although the choice of metre, as I have already argued, is in itself a strong indication of a date not earlier than the fourth century. Lack of material precludes a more precise conclusion, except that the death of Fulgentius (A.D. 550) can be accepted as a safe *terminus ante quem* for the composition of the *P.V.* Fulgentius' tetrameters are metrically barbarous, but two of his purer lines are remarkably similar to line 19-20 of the *P.V.* (cf. notes *ad loc.*). Clearly Fulgentius has borrowed these lines, with adaptations, from a poet who knew his metre ; this explains their relative purity and these can be no question of the poet of the *P.V.* being the imitator.

Pervigilium Veneris

Cras amet qui numquam amavit quique amavit cras amet.

> ver novum, ver iam canorum ; vere natus orbis est,
> vere concordant amores, vere nubunt alites,
> et nemus comam resolvit de maritis imbribus.
> 5   cras amorum copulatrix inter umbras arborum
> implicat casas virentis de flagello myrteo,
> cras Dione iura dicit fulta sublimi throno.

cras amet qui numquam amavit quique amavit cras amet.

> . . . .

> tunc cruore de superno spumeo Pontus globo
> 10   caerulas inter catervas, inter et bipedes equos
> fecit undantem Dionem de marinis imbribus.

INCIPIT. PER. VIRGILIUM. VENERIS. TROCAICO. METRO. Sunt vero versus XXII
S : PERVIGILIUM VENERIS INCIPIT V : *omisit* T   1 amavit *pr* : amabit S
amavit cras : cras amavit T   2 vere : ver T   orbis : iovis S   ver renatus orbis
est *Lipsius*   3 amores : amaiores T   nubent T   4 conam resolvet T
5 amorem T   6 casas *Pithoeus* : gaza S : gazas TV   7 fultas S   8 quinque T
    post 8 lacunam indicavit Bergkius   9 tunc SV : tuno T   tum *Cazzaniga*
superbo S : superuo V   quivore de superhuc spumeo pontus de glovo T
10 etui pedes T   11 Dione TV   marinis *Rivinus* : maritis STV   imbribus :
*hanc lectionem fortasse, sicut 'maritis', ex 4 sumptam puto et poetam nostrum 'fluctibus'
scripsisse.*

> Who has never loved shall love tomorrow,
> tomorrow shall love who has loved before.

Spring is new, now spring is full of song ; the world was born in spring, love in
spring is harmony, the birds marry in spring and the grove unbinds her hair to the
5 husband-showers. Tomorrow, in the shade of the trees, the love-binder weaves
her green bowers from shoots of myrtle ; tomorrow Dione proclaims her laws
seated upon her high throne.

> Who has never loved shall love tomorrow,
> tomorrow shall love who has loved before.

> (. . . . .)

10 Then from heaven's blood, in a ball of foam, among azure hosts and two-footed
horses, Pontus made Dione who rose in billows from the waves of the ocean.

cras amet qui numquam amavit quique amavit cras amet.

ipsa gemmis purpurantem pingit annum floridis,
ipsa surgentes papillas de Favoni spiritu
15 urget in nodos tepentes ; ipsa roris lucidi,
noctis aura quem relinquit, spargit umentis aquas.
emicant lacrimae trementes de caduco pondere ;
gutta praeceps orbe parvo sustinet casus suos.
en ! pudorem florulentae prodiderunt purpurae.
20 umor ille, quem serenis astra rorant noctibus,
mane virgineas papillas solvit umenti peplo.
ipsa iussit mane nudae virgines nubant rosae ;
facta Cypridis de cruore deque Amoris osculis
deque gemmis deque flammis deque solis purpuris,
25 cras ruborem, qui latebat veste tectus ignea,
unico marita nodo non pudebit solvere.

13 gemmas T   floridis *Riglerus* : floribus STV   14 Faboni ST   15 nodos tepentes *Lipsius alii alia* : notos penates S : totos pentes T : totos pen^a tes V 16 relinquid T tumentis ST   17 emicant *Statius* : etmicanat S : etmecanat TV lacrimas S   decadum TV   punder V   18 urbe S   sustine S   19 en *Bouhierus* : in STV   pudore S   purpore S : pupure T   20 notibus T 21 virgines V   papilla T   tumenti S   22 ipiussit T   mane nudae *Mackail* (?) *alii alia* : manet tute S : mane tute V : mane tuae T   23 facta S : fusta T : fusta V   Cypridis *Buechelerus alii alia* : prius STV   decque T   osculis S *et Sannazarius* : oculis TV   24 purporis S : pupuris T   26 unico marita nodo *Pithoeus alii alia* : unica marita noto S : unica^at marita nodo V : unica marito nodo T pudent T

Who has never loved shall love tomorrow,
tomorrow shall love who has loved before.

Dione paints the purpling year with glittering flower buds. As the blooms grow
15 under Favonius' breath she drives them against their glowing sheaths ; she scatters the liquid draughts of gleaming dew which the night-wind leaves. Tears flash and tremble with sinking weight : the falling drop's small sphere delays its
20 headlong fall. See ! the crimson flowers have unveiled their blushes ! At dawn the dew, distilled from stars in the tranquil night, will loose their virginal breasts from dripping robes. The goddess has ordered the roses to marry as naked virgins.
25 Made from the Cyprian's blood, from kisses of Amor, from jewels, from fire and from the sun's glory, tomorrow the rose will forget shame and unfold the crimson that has hidden behind a fiery robe ; unashamed, she will dedicate herself in a single marriage-bond.

cras amet qui numquam amavit quique amavit cras amet.

    ipsa nymphas diva luco iussit ire myrteo ;
    it puer comes puellis, nec tamen credi potest
30   esse Amorem feriatum, si sagittas vexerit.
    ite, nymphae, posuit arma, feriatus est Amor !
    iussus est inermis ire, nudus ire iussus est,
    neu quid arcu neu sagitta neu quid igne laederet.
    sed tamen, nymphae, cavete, quod Cupido pulcher est ;
35   totus est in armis idem quando nudus est Amor.

cras amet qui numquam amavit quique amavit cras amet.

    (. . . . .)

    conpari Venus pudore mittit ad te virgines ;
    una res est quam rogamus : cede, virgo Delia,
    ut nemus sit incruentum de ferinis stragibus,
    et rigentibus virentes ducat umbras floribus   (58)

28 luco S *et Sannazarius* : loco TV   iussit : lusit V   29 it *Pithoeus* : et STV
comis TV   31 ite : in te S   32 est : e S   nudos S : durus T
33 acuneo T   digne T   35 in armis *Pithoeus* inermis STV   est in armis totus
Salmasius metri causa, fortasse recte.   sidem S   36 quique : qui T   *post 36*
lacunam indicavit Riese, fortasse recte.   38 unam S   re T   39 nemus S *et*
Sannazarius : nenus T : veͫnus V   incruendum T   tragibus S   *58 huc*
primum transtulit editor Lipsiensis (1872), qui tamen coniecturam Scaligeri male probavit
rigentibus STV : recentibus *Scaliger*   vergentes T : viͬgentes V   vigentibus
virentes *Sannazarius*   duoad umbra S

Who has never loved shall love tomorrow,
tomorrow shall love who has loved before.

The goddess has ordered the nymphs to go to the myrtle grove. The boy
30 accompanies the maidens, but you cannot believe that Love is on holiday if he has
brought his arrows. Go, nymphs, he has laid down his arms : Love is on holiday !
He was ordered to go weaponless, to go naked, that he might do no harm with
either his bow, his arrow or his torch. But, nymphs, beware, for Cupid is
35 beautiful, and Love, when naked, is in full panoply.

Who has never loved shall love tomorrow,
tomorrow shall love who has loved before.

    (. . . . .)

Venus sends you virgins, modest as yourself, Delian. One thing we ask : go, virgin

40 ipsa vellet te rogare si pudicam flecteret ;
    ipsa vellet ut venires, si deceret virginem.
    iam tribus choros videres feriatis noctibus
    congreges inter catervas ire per saltus tuos,
    floreas inter coronas, myrteas inter casas.
45 nec Ceres, nec Bacchus absunt nec poetarum deus.
    detinenda tota nox est, pervigilanda canticis ;
    regnet in silvis Dione, tu recede Delia !

cras amet qui numquam amavit quique amavit cras amet.

    iussit Hyblaeis tribunal stare diva floribus ;
50 praeses ipsa iura dicit, adsederunt Gratiae.
    Hybla totos funde flores, quidquid annus adtulit,
    Hybla florum sume vestem, quantus Aetnae campus est !
    ruris hic erunt puellae, vel puellae montium :
    quaeque silvas, quaeque lucos, quaeque fontes incolunt ;

40 *omisit* T   vellit S   te rogare *Salmasius* : erogare SV   41 vellit S
diceret T   42 chorus S *fortasse recte*   43 *post 'congreges' desinit* A
44 myrteo S   misteas T   45 baccas T   potearum S   deas T
46 detinenda *Heinsius* : detinente S : detinent et TV   pervigilanda *scripsi* :
perviclanda S : pervigila TV   49 Hyblei S   50 praeses *Scaliger* : praesens STV
dicit adsederunt STV : dicet adsidebunt *Dousa senior*   51 totus S   fundet S
qui 'flores' omisit   annus *Sannazarius* : annos S : annis TV   52 sume vestem
Heinsius alii alia : superestem S : rumpe TV reste T : restem V   Aetnae V : etnec S :
ethne T   53 montium STV : fontium *Sannazarius*   54 quaeque (*alt.*) : quae S :
que T   locus S : locos T   queque (*tert.*) ST   fontes *Scriverius* : montes STV

40 of Delos, leave the forest, unstained by the slaughter of wild beasts, to trace verdant shadows over upright flowers. Gladly would she have invited you, if she could bend your chaste heart, gladly have willed your company, if that became a virgin ; through three nights of festival you would now have seen bands of dancers wandering through your glades, among massed crowds, amidst bowers
45 of myrtle and coronals of flowers. Nor are Ceres or Bacchus absent, nor the patron god of poets. The whole night is to be filled, kept vigil with song. Let Dione reign in the woodlands, Delian depart !

Who has never loved shall love tomorrow,
tomorrow shall love who has loved before.

The goddess has ordered her tribunal to stand among flowers of Hybla. She
50 herself presides and proclaims her laws ; the Graces have taken their seats. Hybla,

55   iussit omnes adsidere pueri mater alitis,
         iussit et nudo puellas nil Amori credere.

cras amet qui numquam amavit quique amavit cras amet.

         cras erit quo primus Aether copulavit nuptias ;
60   ut pater totum crearet vernis annum nubibus,
         in sinum maritus imber fluxit almae coniugis,
         unde fetus mixtus omnis aleret magno corpore.
         ipsa venas atque mentem permeanti spiritu
         intus occultis gubernat procreatrix viribus,
65   perque caelum perque terras perque pontum subditum
         pervium sui tenorem seminali tramite
         imbuit iussitque mundum nosse nascendi vias.

cras amet qui numquam amavit quique amavit cras amet.

         ipsa Troianos nepotes in Latinos transtulit ;

55 alitis S *et Sannazarius* : alitas TV   56 nullo T   amoti T   59 quo SV : qui T : quom *Buechelerus et alii*   60 totum *Salmasianus* : totis STV   creavit S   61 fluxit : fluctus T   alma et T : almae et V   62 unde S : ut TV   flaetus S : fletus T   alteret S   63 vernas T   adque S   64 procreatis S   65 perque (*pr.*) : perquem ST   perque (*alt.*) : perquem S   66 tenderem S   67 nosce T   69 nepotes : nec potes T   latino TV

pour forth the year's whole harvest of flowers ! Hybla, plait a garland of flowers as wide as the plain of Aetna ! The nymphs of field and mountain will be here : all
55 who live in forest, grove or fountain. The mother of the winged child has ordered all to be seated, and bidden the maidens to have no trust in Amor, even when he is naked.

Who has never loved shall love tomorrow,
tomorrow shall love who has loved before.

60 Tomorrow is the day when Ether first coupled in nuptial union. That, as father, he might create the whole year from clouds of spring, the husband shower fell into the lap of his fecund bride, so that, joined to her mighty body, he might sustain all life. She, the creatress, with permeant spirit and hidden strength,
65 governs within both blood and mind ; in the passage of the seed she has eternally impressed her pervasive immanence upon sky, land and sea ; she has ordered the world to know the ways of birth.

Who has never loved shall love tomorrow,
tomorrow shall love who has loved before.

70   ipsa Laurentem puellam coniugem nato dedit ;
       moxque Marti de sacello dat pudicam virginem ;
       Romuleas ipsa fecit cum Sabinis nuptias,
       unde Ramnes et Quirites proque prole posterum
       † Romuli matrem † crearet et nepotem Caesarem.

75 cras amet qui numquam amavit quique amavit cras amet.

       rura fecundat voluptas, rura Venerem sentiunt,
       ipse Amor, puer Dionae, rure natus dicitur.
       hunc, ager cum parturiret, ipsa suscepit sinu,
       ipsa florum delicatis educavit osculis.

80 cras amet qui numquam amavit quique amavit cras amet.

       ecce iam subter genestas explicant tauri latus,
       quisque tutus quo tenetur coniugali foedere ;
       subter umbras cum maritis ecce balantum greges ;
       et canoras non tacere diva iussit alites :
85   iam loquaces ore rauco stagna cycni perstrepunt,

       70 ipa S   72 ipsas S   Saumis T   73 Samnes S : rames T
       74 Romuli, patrem *Lipsius alii alia*   76 facundat T   77 natu S
       78 perturiret TV   sinum S   79 deligatis S   80 quique amat T
       81 subter *Broukhusius* : super STV   explicant tauri *Scaliger* : explicat aonii STV :
       agni *Lipsius*   82 tuus TV   cum iugali T   83 valantum T   gregum TV
       84 canores T   85 stangna S   cygni : quinni S

70 It was she who made Latins of her Trojan descendants, she who gave the girl of
    Laurentum as wife to her son ; soon afterwards from the sanctuary she gave the
    chaste virgin to Mars. It was she who made the marriage of Romulus' men with
    the Sabines, that, from their union, she might create the Ramnes, the Quirites,
75 and, for later generations, † the mother of Romulus † and Caesar, the grandson.

       Who has never loved shall love tomorrow,
       tomorrow shall love who has loved before.

Delight quickens the fields, the fields sense Venus' power. Love himself, the child
of Dione is said to have been born in the fields. While the land was in labour, she
80 took him to her breast and nourished him upon the tender kisses of flowers.

       Who has never loved shall love tomorrow,
       tomorrow shall love who has loved before.

See ! the bulls now stretch their flanks under the broom trees, each secure in his
binding love-union. Under the shadows of the trees see ! the bleating flocks with
85 their mates. The goddess has ordered the song-birds not to cease their melody, the

adsonat Terei puella subter umbram populi,
ut putes motus amoris ore dici musico,
et neges queri sororem de marito barbaro.
illa cantat, nos tacemus ; quando ver venit meum ?
90   quando fiam uti chelidon, ut tacere desinam ?
perdidi musam tacendo, nec me Phoebus respicit.
sic Amyclas, cum tacerent, perdidit silentium.

cras amet qui numquam amavit quique amavit cras amet.

86 adsonante aerei T   puellae TV   supter T   87 putes S *et Sannazarius* :
putas TV   88 eet T   queris S   89 quan vir venit S   90 fiam S : faciam
TV   uti *Rivinus* : ut STV   taceret T   91 perdidimus an tacendo TV   ne
V   92 amidas T   taceret ST   perdedit S

EXPLICIT PER VIRGILIUM VENERIS T

marshes now resound with the raucous chatter of the swans, while Tereus' girl
sings in the shadows ; you would think she was singing the melodious motions of
90 love, and deny that her sister laments a brutal lord. She sings, I am silent. When
will I become like the swallow and cease my silence ? Through silence I have
destroyed my muse, Phoebus ignores me. So silence destroyed mute Amyclae.

Who has never loved shall love tomorrow,
tomorrow shall love who has loved before.

Notes

In the following notes I have aimed at three complementary objectives : to justify my text, interpret the Latin as precisely and accurately as possible, and to provide some indication of the place and stature of the *Pervigilium* in the tradition of Latin poetry. Textual discussion and exegesis is found in the notes on individual lines or line-groups, while, in the introduction to each stanza, I outline the traditions upon which the poet is drawing, his contribution to these traditions, and the conceptual function of each stanza within the plan of the poem as a whole. Stylistic criticism, except where it is of textual significance or relevant to the problems of date and authorship, has been largely excluded beyond some general remarks in the introduction to stanza I, and occasional remarks elsewhere in the notes. It has been a constant struggle to keep this edition within modest bounds, and I have therefore decided to leave the reader to form his own estimate of the poet's technical mastery. The metre is discussed in a separate section ; my impression of the poet's metrical achievement can be found in its concluding paragraphs.

A brief postscript follows the notes, in which I have attempted a final statement of the achievement of the poem and its claim to be regarded as serious and important literature.

Stanza I : Spring

'With the exception of the *Pervigilium Veneris*', wrote Helen Waddell, 'the spring song scarcely exists in Latin literature'. Of lyric this is true. Catullus has left us a short poem (XLVI) which communicates his experience of spring ; it is the record of a mounting impulse in both mind and body, an impulse which provokes a longing for travel and adventure ; of love not a word. Three Horatian odes (I, 4 ; IV, 7, 12) grow from spring landscapes, but, in all of them, spring is conceived in terms of its virtual opposite, Winter, and, although, in I, 4, we meet a brief and oblique reference to love, Horace's response to spring is nothing like the unqualified optimism of the first stanza of the *Pervigilium* ; it is a sombre insistence upon the flight of time and upon human mortality :

> *immortalia ne speres monet annus et almum*
> *quae rapit hora diem.*   (IV, 7, 5-6)

From the lyric tradition a poem by Pentadius in epanaleptic couplets (*A.L.* 235) perhaps most nearly approaches the P.V. in its treatment of the spring-motif. The poem evokes the swelling life, the tumult and fervour of spring, but culminates with the poet's prayer for an ecstatic *Liebestod* in a shadowed retreat. This note of melancholy has already been conveyed by Philomela's song (7-8) and by Echo's haunting call (13-14), but in the closing couplet we realise that sadness lies at the heart of Pentadius' experience of spring.

It is true that pain is to darken the radiant vision of the *Pervigilium*, but there is no hint of it here in the opening stanza, which is closer to treatments of spring and love in didactic or religious poetry than to anything in personal lyric. This is hardly surprising, as the *Pervigilium Veneris* is a quasi-liturgical celebration of Venus' dynamic presence at every level of creation. Personal feeling, although implicit throughout, only emerges openly in the concluding lines of the poem.

In the fourth book of the *Fasti* Ovid glorifies spring as preeminently the season of Venus :

> *nec Veneri tempus quam ver erat aptius ullum,*
> *vere nitent terrae, vere remissus ager.*
> *nunc herbae rupta tellure cacumina tollunt,*
> *nunc tumido gemmas cortice palmes agit ;*
> *et formosa Venus formoso tempore digna est,*
> *utque solet, Marti continuata suo est.*
> *vere monet curvas materna per aequora puppes*
> *ire nec hibernas iam timuisse minas.*   (125-32)

Comparison reveals the strength of the *Pervigilium*, especially in its use of repetition, a technique which is used neatly by Ovid, but without the same feeling of compressed and mounting excitement ; this is because it is not accompanied by significant conceptual growth :

> *ver novum, ver iam canorum ; vere natus orbis est,*
> *vere concordant amores, vere nubunt alites.*
> *et nemus comam resolvit de maritis imbribus.*

Repetition here is dynamic because each instance, strengthened by assonance and alliteration, introduces a new idea : the freshness of spring,

song, birth, harmony, love and marriage ; a whole complex of ideas, which represent the germ of the entire poem, are introduced in these lines, while personification, first apparent in *nubunt*, and used to develop the beautiful metaphor of the following line, reveals a more complex attitude to, and involvement in, the processes of nature than is apparent in Ovid's spring song ; for I do not feel that Ovid seriously links repetition with the communication of new ideas : it is far more like mere technique or a means of developing a basically facile argument (*formosa Venus formoso tempore digna*).

What is so impressive in the *Pervigilium* is the poet's control ; avoiding the purely decorative he concentrates on what he considers important ; ignoring the accidents of spring he stresses its significant qualities. Spring is far more than a charming landscape ; it is the shared experience of a sentient world.

Like the later poet of the *Pervigilium* Lucretius, in the magnificent exordium to book one of the *De Rerum Natura*, celebrates spring as a universal response to the power of Venus, the expression in landscape, body and mind of her pervasive immanence :

> *te dea, te fugiunt venti, te nubila caeli*
> *adventumque tuum, tibi suavis daedala tellus*
> *summittit flores, tibi rident aequora ponti*
> *placatumque nitet diffuso lumine caelum.*
> *nam simul ac species patefactast verna diei*
> *et reserata viget genitabilis aura favoni,*
> *aeriae primum volucres te, diva, tuumque*
> *significant initum perculsae corda tua vi.*
> *inde ferae pecudes persultant pabula laeta*
> *et rapidos tranant amnis : ita capta lepore*
> *te sequitur cupide quo quamque inducere pergis.*
> *denique per maria ac montes fluviosque rapacis*
> *frondiferasque domos avium camposque virentis*
> *omnibus incutiens blandum per pectora amorem*
> *efficis ut cupide generatim saecla propagent.*   (6-20)

As a goddess of creative power and harmony Lucretius implores Venus' patronage for his bold venture (21-7), as a goddess of peace her favour is asked for the Roman people (29-40). Lucretius' Venus shares these attributes with the Venus of the *Pervigilium Veneris*, but, without implying a value-judgment, I would point out the following differences in the two poets' practice : that Lucretius' method is more decorative, and that his portrayal of Venus' activity in creation is of a more vehement force provoking a more impetuous response than the impression of her influence conveyed by the poet of the *Pervigilium*, who deliberately avoids the emotional implications of participles like *perculsae* and *capta* or of adverbs like *cupide*. Of course Venus, in Lucretius, is no more than a poetic realisation of atomic theory ; she represents the compelling physical force which drives atoms into creative union, while her lover, Mars, personifies the opposing tendency towards atomic disruption. Their liaison symbolises the ἰσονομία, the finely balanced yet shifting poise of the universe. The speed and urgency of atomic movement is, for Lucretius, one of the wonders of creation, which both explains and justifies the emotional tenor of his invocation. But, in the *Pervigilium*, Venus is far more than a metaphor for a physical phenomenon ; she is the spirit and meaning of life, the Queen of the heart as well as of nature. Hence the poet suppresses suggestions of violent emotion or passion and presents her influence as a pressure towards harmony, love and marriage.

The description of spring in Book X of Columella's *De Re Rustica* is of little poetic value, but very clearly illustrates what the poet of the *Pervigilium* avoids :

> *nunc sunt genitalia tempora mundi,*
> *nunc amor ad coitus properat, nunc spiritus orbis*
> *bacchatur Veneri stimulisque cupidinis actus*
> *ipse suos adamat partus et partibus implet.*   (196-9)

Note the verb *bacchatur* and the use of the phrase *stimulis cupidinis* to describe the force of love. Columella continues to relate how the sea-gods violate (*polluere*) their wives (200-3), how Jupiter descends as a deceitful and incestuous adulterer into the lap of his libidinous parent (204-8) :

> *hinc maria, hinc montes, hinc totus denique mundus*
> *ver agit, hinc hominum pecudum volucrumque cupido*
> *atque amor ignescit menti saevitque medullis.*   (212-14)

This is not a picture of universal harmony, but an evocation of un-controllable cosmic lust which is quite remote from the power of love glorified in the *Pervigilium*, for there nature's sexuality is exalted as a transcendent moral influence which vivifies and unites the whole of creation.

I hope these poetic contrasts help towards an understanding of our poet's presentation of spring, particularly in his rejection of pure description in favour of a metaphorical and conceptual emphasis, an emphasis which equates love, not with elegiac frenzy, but with harmony and marriage. I have discussed these lines at length because the qualities they embody are features of the whole poem, illustrating the poet's original and imaginative reshaping of the traditions he inherited.

To the spring-motif and its associations line 5 adds a note of joyful expectation : *cras*. Tomorrow is a day of high festival, tomorrow Dione proclaims her laws. The *Pervigilium*, I think, shares this feeling of glad anticipation with the epithalamic tradition, indeed in stanza VII *cras* is celebrated as the wedding-day of all creation. But it is not only the feeling of expectation which reminds me of an *epithalamium* but also the poet's insistence on the morality and security of sexual union, ideas which are suggested here in Stanza I and are to be developed more explicitly in the following stanzas (cf. esp. introduction to stanzas III and IV).

Sunt vero versus XXII. This is part of the superscription in S and has been wrongly interpreted by several editors as evidence for the original stanzaic pattern of the *Pervigilium*, an error in which Mackail (1912) and Fort persisted long after Riese, in his introduction to the *Anthologia* (XVIII ff.), proved that *versus* refers, not to the number of verses in the *Pervigilium*, but to the number of poems in that section of S which begins with the *P.V.*

1. *Cras amet*, etc. Clementi here omits the refrain as part of his strophic reorganisation. He justifies this by reference to Erasmus' description of the poem as a *carmen de vere*, arguing that *ver* must have been the first word of the *Pervigilium* in Erasmus' text. This is a highly questionable assumption, but even assuming its validity, it suggests only that the first line had been omitted by a copyist and tells us nothing about the true first line of the *Pervigilium*.

The refrain is employed at irregular intervals throughout the poem, and Schilling refers to analogies for such a usage in Greek and Latin bucolic verse. I would mention also the *Dirae* and the *Lydia*, where something approaching a refrain appears as an irregular feature of structure, but the text itself is its own best justification, where every stanza develops particular aspects of the festival and where the refrain thus punctuates the conceptual movement of the poem ; it is used, not to establish a symmetrical verse-pattern, but to emphasise the poet's universal summons where the sense makes this appropriate.

Among recent editors Schilling, Romano and Cazzaniga all preserve the MSS structure of the *Pervigilium* as a poem divided by the refrain into stanzas of unequal length. Now that the meaning of the superscription in

S has been understood, there is no reason for the complex reorganisations of Clementi and others (cf. Clementi 57-65) ; transpositions and lacunas postulated in search of strophic symmetry are without justification.

2. *ver ... ver ... vere .... vere*. The poet is expanding Virg., *Georg.* II, 323-4 :

> *ver adeo frondi nemorum, ver utile silvis,*
> *vere tument terrae et genitalia semina poscunt.*

Repetition at once emerges as a feature of the poem. The key words are *ver, maritus, cras* and *ipsa*, used with the force of Wagnerian *Leitmotiv* to drive home the poet's preoccupations.

vere natus orbis est : the reading of V (*vere natus iovis* S, *ver natus orbis* T), but Lipsius' *ver renatus orbis est* demands careful consideration, particularly since the opening lines in general represent the poet's response to the immediate facts of spring, to the here-and-now of life, rather than a statement of spring's primeval significance. In this context the joyous affirmation, 'spring is the world reborn', is perhaps more appropriate than the tamer reflection, 'the world was born in spring'. The fact that the poet, in stanzas 2 and 8, where he is thinking specifically of *cras*, develops aspects of the festival's historical importance, is no sure guide to his intentions here, where he is writing more generally about spring. Nor does literary tradition provide any clear indication of the reading, as other poets freely associate spring with both cosmic rebirth and primal generation (cf. Clementi *ad loc.*). I incline to *vere natus* because it is the reading of both S and V, for what that is worth when it is remembered that MSS were copied without regard for word division, and because the progression from double to triple repetition is rhetorically more satisfying.

Clementi compares the idea (*vere natus orbis est*) with Chrysipp. fr. 584 (Arnim vol. II, p. 180) and comments : 'Stoic philosophy held that the world was born in spring', but I do not think that we are necessarily dealing, in the *Pervigilium*, with a conscious use of Stoic ideas rather than with a tradition which, by the time of late antiquity, was common to several philosophical systems. Cf., for example, Ambrose, *Hex.* I, 4, 13 (on God's creation of the world) : *in hoc ergo principio mensium caelum et terram fecit, quod inde mundi capi oportebat exordium, ubi erat oportuna omnibus verna temperies, unde et annus mundi imaginem nascentis expressit, ut post hibernas glacies verni temporis splendor eluceat.*

The influence of Stoicism on the thought of the *Pervigilium* has, in my opinion, been over-emphasised, cf. my introduction and notes to stanza VII.

3. *concordant* : this verb, rare in the classical era, became increasingly popular in late antiquity, especially with patristic authors (cf. *Thes. s.v.*). It can be interpreted in two ways here, meaning either that a) Love is an emotion appropriate to the season of spring ; or b) in springtime love-affairs are harmonious. Perhaps both senses are intended with the emphasis on b).

nubunt. Lewis and Short classify this usage of *nubere* as generalised, which is incorrect, for *nubere* is used here with its customary meaning referring to a woman taking a husband, just as there is no generalised notion in 22 where the *rosae* are personified as young maidens. But for *nubere* of men, cf. Non., 143, 23 : *nubere veteres non solum mulieres sed etiam viros dicebant, ita ut nunc Itali dicunt.* Nonius wrote in the fourth century and may therefore have been a contemporary of our poet. Cf. also Tertullian, *ad Uxor.* I, 7 : *Pontificem Maximum rursus nubere nefas est ; ibid.* II, 11 : *nec filii sine consensu patrum rite et iure nubent.* But that *nubere* here is employed with its usual emphasis is confirmed by the context of line 4, where our attention is concentrated upon the *nemus* as the bride of the *mariti imbres.*

4. *comam resolvit. Coma*, used to describe the foliage of trees, is common enough (e.g. Cat., IV, 12 ; Tib., I, 4, 30 ; Hor., IV, 7, 2), but its use here is particularly imaginative, personifying the grove as a maiden unloosing her hair to the embrace of the husband showers (for this interpretation of *maritis*, cf. further note on this line *s.v.*).

de. Our poet is inordinately fond of this preposition ; I tabulate his usage as follows :

   1) *de loco* : 11, 71.
   2) *de origine* : 6, 9, 23-24 (4 times).
   3) *de causa* : 4, 14, 17, 39.
   4) *de relatione* : 88.

All these instances can be paralleled in the classical poets (cf. *Thes. s.v.*) although the poet's attachment to 3) is particularly idiosyncratic.

Brakman (1928) put forward the use of *de* in the *Pervigilium* as support for his theory that the poem belongs to the age and circle of Q. Aurelius Symmachus. Certainly the poet's eccentric fondness for this preposition suggests a date well into the post-classical era, but it is not specific usages of *de* which are significant so much as his insistent choice of it in preference to alternative constructions, and a brief glance at the pages of Ausonius or Symmachus clearly shows how this feature of our poet's style sets him apart from, rather than connects him with, the circle of Symmachus.

It is by turning to Augustine's psalm against the Donatists that we find a similar affection for *de* : 28 appearances in 275 lines (excluding the refrain) while, with the refrain, the average occurrence of *de* rises to approximately once every four lines. The same stylistic trait is encountered in the work of Fulgentius Ruspensis (467-532 A.D.) who follows Augustine's precedent of attacking heresy by writing a popular psalm, a poem of 294 lines (without the refrain) in which *de* occurs 21 times.

The psalm against the Donatists belongs to the last years of the fourth century (cf. *Augustini scripta contra Donatistas pars I*, ed. M. Petschenig (Leipzig (1908), VI), while Fulgentius wrote about a century later ; moreover Augustine has left us (*Retractiones*, I, 19) a record of the principles which guided his composition of this psalm : *volens etiam causam Donatistarum ad ipsius humillimi vulgi et omnino imperitorum atque idiotarum notitiam pervenire, et eorum quantum fieri posset per nos inhaerere memoriae, psalmum qui eis cantaretur, per Latinas litteras feci.*

This is important. Augustine, an African writer of the fourth century, writing verse in a deliberately popular style, makes insistent use of the preposition *de*, a precedent which is followed by the later apologist, Fulgentius. Note, too, how both writers employ a refrain. Of course the gulf which separates these two pieces from the *Pervigilium* is immense ; in the psalms the line is built around a fixed number of syllables, whereas in the *Pervigilium* it is divided into metrical feet, but the common features which I have stressed, the use of a refrain and, more notably, the continual appearance of *de*, must be considered in any discussion of the date and origin of the *Pervigilium*. They also perhaps cast some light on the poet's intentions ; are the refrain and the use of *de* taken from a genuinely popular tradition to lend an air of 'folk-song' to a sophisticated literary creation ?

de maritis imbribus. The implicit personification of the grove as a young bride unbinding her hair invites a similar interpretation of *maritis* as an appositional noun (cf. *virgines rosae*, line 19) meaning 'husband' showers. I do not believe that *maritus* is used in the *Pervigilium* as an adjective with the post-classical meaning, 'fertile' ; cf. my note on the corrupt MSS reading *maritis imbribus* at line 11.

5. *copulatrix* : a very rare post-classical word, cf. Aug., *Trin*. XI, 7 ; XI, 9.

6. *casas*. Pithou's emendation is confirmed by 44, *myrteas inter casas*. For
these bowers as part of the ritual of the *Pervigilium*, see, 'the Festival',
pp. 27-8.
implicat casas virentis ... Note how the power of the love-binder is
symbolically represented here, as she binds together the tender green
shoots of her sacred myrtle to weave the bowers where the mysteries of
love will be consummated.

7. *Dione*. A tradition of Greek mythology accommodated the originally
foreign Aphrodite into the Olympian pantheon (cf. Eur., *Hel.* 1098 ; Plat.,
Symp. 180 d) as the daughter of Zeus and Dione, the shadowy consort of
the King of Heaven later ousted by Hera. Such a version of the goddess'
birth would of course be anathema in the *Pervigilium* which celebrates the
birthday of Ἀφροδίτη ἀναδυομένη. But throughout Latin literature *Dione* is
also used as a synonym for Venus, a usage particularly common in later
Latin (e.g. Tiberianus, *Carm.* I, 10 ; Nemes, *Ecl.* II, 56 ; Sidon., *Carm.* IX,
173). Schilling is therefore right to insist that the designation *Dione* tells us
nothing about the poet's conception of the love-goddess ; it reflects
metrical convenience and literary fashion.
dicit : praesens pro futuro, cf. notes on line 50.
fulta sublimi throno. Cf. also 49 and my discussion of these lines under
'the Festival' p. 26.
throno : a graecism, cf. Pliny, XXXV, 9 ; Prud., *Hamart.* praef., 10.

Stanza II : the Birth of Venus

In broad outline the poet follows the Hesiodic tradition in his allusion
to the birth of Venus from blood and foam (for differences in the two
poets' treatment cf. notes to line 9) ; other writers make the sea her sole
parent. Our poet's insistence upon Uranus' unwitting participation in the
creation of Venus is rooted in his deepest preoccupations ; for in stanza I
the showers, falling from above, wake the forest to life, while in stanza
VII the primeval wedding of earth and sky is described. The poem as a
whole hymns the glory of union at every level of creation. For this reason
Venus' birth is portrayed as itself a result of the cosmic process which she
inspires and which the poem celebrates.

9. *tunc*. The sudden move from anticipation of *cras* to the statement that
'then the sea created Dione', the chronological confusion which this
abrupt jump seems to involve, has disturbed most editors from Bergk

onwards. But, in spite of the brisk modulation, the sequence of ideas is obvious. We are being told why tomorrow is so high a day of festival : it is the day when Venus was born from blood and sea-spray.

Many editors have eased the progression to *tunc* by transposition. Mackail (1912) inserts line 59 as the first line of this stanza, while Buecheler and Clementi import 59-62 (for other proposals, cf. Clementi 66-8). But the *Pervigilium* celebrates Venus as the mother of all life ; she is the *procreatrix* who has ordered the world to experience the ways of birth (67). Lines 59-62 are correctly placed by the MSS as the beginning of a stanza which glorifies Venus as the universal mother. The transpositions of Mackail and Buecheler distort this fundamental concept by making the birth of the *procreatrix* herself virtually attendant upon the cosmic process she is supposed to have inspired.

Owen, who preserves the MSS line-order, identifies *ver*, not *cras*, as the antecedent of *tunc*. He writes, 'it is true that we have to go to *ver* in line 2, "in spring Venus was born from seafoam", but I see no difficulty in this ; the burden of the poem is spring, the poet's mind is full of spring and he can safely trust the intelligent reader to interpret *tunc* correctly'. But Clementi (p. 49) writes, 'no doubt the poet's mind was full of spring, but this can scarcely have induced him to conceal his meaning by dislocation of adverbs'. As the emphatically repeated *cras* of 5, 7-8 clearly indicates, *tunc* refers specifically to *cras* not more widely to *ver*, and introduces the explanation of tomorrow's significance. To justify the transmitted text we must assume an associative development of ideas, by which the poet turns straight from anticipation of *cras* to the mythological events which make it so important. I am not convinced that this represents an impossible transition, and it is as well to remember that most editors have found their difficulties with *tunc* decidedly useful as an expedient for reorganising the text in their false search for strophic regularity or correspondence.

But although *tunc* is not necessarily an impossible poetic shorthand for *cras erit quo* (cf. 59), stanza II, while arguably the most important stanza in the *P.V.*, in that it explains the momentous significance of tomorrow, is also the shortest. We might expect the poet to dwell at greater length upon the birth of his goddess. Note, moreover, how the sense of every other stanza (not excluding stanza V, where I suspect, however, that several lines have been lost before 37) is completely self-contained ; this can scarcely be a coincidence ; the poet seeems to have writen his stanzas as independent statements of Venus' activity in creation. Stanza II, where the initial *tunc* must be interpreted with reference to the preceding stanza or the preceding refrain, is the only exception to this feature of structure. *Tunc* has now become deeply disturbing ; as the first word of a stanza it introduces an abrupt and difficult transition, but, even more significantly, its grammatical antecedent lies outside its own stanza, which appears to violate the principle of stanzaic self-sufficiency followed elsewhere in the poem. Add these considerations to the surprising brevity of so important a stanza and I believe that Bergk's lacuna has been proved beyond reasonable doubt, especially as the omission explains itself so easily ; for I would suggest that the second stanza, like the seventh, originally began with *cras*, if not with *cras erit quo*, and that the lost line went on to explain that tomorrow will be the anniversary of Venus' birth ; but the scribe of our archetype, seduced by the initial *cras*, mistook this line for the refrain he had just copied, passed straight to *tunc* and thus perpetrated a minor tragedy of omission.

Cazzaniga's *tum*, for the MSS *tunc*, is much smoother before the consonants of *cruore*, and is not fundamentally unlikely ; but we must remember that *tunc* is commoner than *tum* in post-classical Latin (the reason for their constant confusion), and that *tunc* may here retain some of its original emphatic force.

cruore de superno spumeo pontus globo : an allusive reference to the matter from which Venus was created. Hesiod describes (*Theogn*. 188-92) how the genitals of the mutilated Uranus were cast into the sea and formed a white foam in which the goddess took shape. Schilling writes, 'le poète a suivi Hésiode, tout en accordant un rôle important à l'écume marine'. But Cazzaniga (58-9) points out the differences between the two treatments : how, in Hesiod (183-7) the blood of Uranus falls on the earth to engender the Erinyes, Giants and Nymphs, whereas Venus is born from his genitals and not, as in the *P.V.*, from his blood ; how the *Pervigilium* represents the sea (*pontus*) as the active agent of Venus' birth, whereas in Hesiod she grows within the foam which gathers around the flesh of the god. Cazzaniga refers the modification of the myth in the *Pervigilium* to Greek sources, a reasonable assumption for an editor who dates the poem to the second century. But if I am right in following those scholars who place the *Pervigilium* not earlier than the fourth century, it would be rash to presuppose direct influence from a Greek source. We need a Latin tradition ; cf., Apuleius, *Met*. IV, 28 (describing how Psyche's beauty was thought to be a divine manifestation) : *fama pervaserat deam, quam caerulum profundum pelagi peperit et ros spumantium fluctuum educavit, iam numinis sui passim tributa venia in mediis conversari populi coetibus, vel certe rursum novo caelestium stillarum germine, non maria sed terras Venerem aliam virginali flore praeditam pullulasse.*

10. *caerulas inter catervas.* An imprecise phrase, the evocative power of which resides precisely in its deliberately ambiguous impressionism.

bipedes equos : Schilling compares the expression with Virg., *Georg.* IV, 338-9 :

> *caeruleus Proteus, magnum qui piscibus aequor*
> *et iuncto bipedum curru metitur equorum.*

Note the dactylic 6th foot.

undantem de marinis imbribus. The MSS all read *maritis imbribus. Maritus* is certainly a favourite word of the poet and is used five times elsewhere, where its meaning, however, is always 'husband', 'wife' or 'lover' (cf. notes to lines 4, 26, 61, 88). It cannot easily support a related meaning here, where it must, if retained, be taken as an adjective meaning 'potent' or 'fertile'. Corruption is therefore suggested by the poet's own usage, while the reading is made doubly suspect by the further consideration that *de maritis imbribus* represents no more than an unnecessary, and less precise, reformulation of *cruore de superno spumeo globo.* Paraphrase emphasises how unsatisfactory *maritis* is : 'the sea from heavenly blood, in a ball of foam, fashioned Dione, who rose from the potent showers (i.e. the commingled blood and foam)'. Reading *marinis* we can translate as follows : 'from heavenly blood the sea made Dione rise in a ball of foam from the waves of the ocean'. This seems to me so much more natural, more elegant and more satisfying that it is almost certainly what the poet intended. Rivinus' emendation *marinis* is accepted with confidence. I also suspect that *imbribus* needs correction, that it has been imported from line 4 as a consequence of the initial misreading of *marinis*, and that the poet originally wrote *de marinis fluctibus.* Repetition, of course, is a feature of the poet's technique, but is usually dynamic, helping to create the atmosphere of excitement and expectancy which pervades the poem. I cannot see how the reappearance of *imbribus* here contributes to such a feeling and prefer to regard it as an intrusion due to scribal error rather than as an unimaginative repetition of the poet himself.

Schilling, reading *marinis*, interprets the phrase as describing how Dione was born over the sea towards Paphos : 'elle est portée sur les flots de la mer'. But the force of *de* is here far more easily taken as one of origin, indicating where she rose from rather than what she rode upon.

Dionem. Most editors correct the orthography of S to give a Greek accusative, *Dionen*, but I see no reason for assuming a perfect classical standard in the spelling of Greek proper nouns.

undantem : used with a truly Horatian *curiosa felicitas* to suggest the swaying grace of the spray-blown, sinuous goddess rising from the waves.

Stanza III : the Rose

In the first two stanzas spring has been associated with primal genesis, with song, harmony and marriage. Tomorrow has been proclaimed a festival of love in honour of the birth of Venus. The poet now moves from his statement of these primary motifs to their development, evoking the expression of Venus' power in the tissue of creation, in the world of bud and flower. As befits development the texture is richer and more colourful, although description still serves a conceptual and metaphorical purpose, for the swelling roses are symbolic virgins, cherished by Venus and soon to surrender to her power in sexual dedication.

This is not the first Latin poet for whom the unplucked flower has symbolised virginity ; Catullus LXII is a wedding song, an exchange between a chorus of youths, asserting the rights of the *maritus*, and a choir of maidens who seek to preserve the innocence of the young *nupta*. In stanza VII the bride is compared with a tender flower :

> *ut flos in saeptis secretus nascitur hortis,*
> *ignotus pecori, nullo convolsus aratro,*
> *quem mulcent aurae, firmat sol, educat imber ;*
> *multi illum pueri, multae optavere puellae :*
> *idem cum tenui carptus defloruit ungui,*
> *nulli illum pueri, nullae optavere puellae :*
> *sic virgo, dum intacta manet, dum cara suis est ;*
> *cum castum amisit polluto corpore florem,*
> *nec pueris iucunda manet, nec cara puellis.*   (39-47)

The simile illustrates the virgins' conception of sexual union as an act of violation and irrevocable loss. In reply the chorus of youths contrast a sterile, creeping vine, ignored by the farmer and his team, with the same vine when joined to the elm ; the fruitful intercourse of vine and elm is used to justify the sexual assertion of the *maritus* ; simile expresses, but does not reconcile, conflicting ideas and emotions. The final stanza (59-66) implies little change of feeling on the bride's part ; she is urged not to struggle against the man her parents have chosen, and reminded that she does not possess sole rights over her own virginity. The unsullied flower, which the virgin so prizes, must still be plucked and her sense of loss, in unwilling submission, still remains.

A group of poems in the *Anthologia Latina* treat the swift unfolding and fall of rose blossoms as a reminder of the transience of youth and beauty ; the plucking of the rose, as in Catullus, is a symbol of sexual pleasure :

> *o quales ego mane rosas procedere vidi !*
> *nascebantur adhuc nec erat par omnibus aetas.*
> *prima papillatos ducebat [tecta] corymbos,*
> *altera puniceos apices umbone levabat,*
> *tertia iam totum calathi patefecerat orbem,*
> *quarta simul nituit nudato germine floris.*
> *dum levat una caput dumque explicat altera nodum,*
> *ac dum virgineus pudor exsinuatur amictu,*
> *ne pereant, lege mane rosas : cito virgo senescit.*   (*A.L.* 84)

This is a pretty poem but, far from the glow and warmth of the *Pervigilium*, a brittle and cold one. The symbolism of the rose is interpreted with cynical detachment : cull your virgins young !

A.L. 646, a longer and more elaborate piece, describes dawn in a rose-garden. It is a riot of colour and growth and sudden decay. The poet creates a scene of magical beauty, but the radiance of dawn and of the vividly personified roses, the sudden surge of life and movement in lines 23-32, only emphasizes the poet's final insistence upon the fragility of the scene he has created. The poem concludes in an explicit analogy with human experience, which reveals its purpose as a veiled invitation to sexual surrender :

> *collige, virgo, rosas, dum flos novus et nova pubes*
> *et memor esto aevum sic properare tuum.*

In these poems the rose functions as a metaphor for impermanence and consequently as an argument for indulgence while youth allows and beauty still invites. The central feature is its plucking, a symbol at once of masculine assertion and of virginal loss. Beyond this limited symbolic purpose, the impact of the poetry resides in descriptive charm which is pursued as an end in itself.

In his development of the rose-motif the poet of the *Pervigilium* displays a marvellous sureness of touch. All the visual details of the stanza are charged with a metaphorical, an emotional significance which communicates a marvellous awakening. Symbolism and description are perfectly harmonised until the metaphor emerges into open dominance from line 22. The *papillae* of line 14 are swelling buds, they are also the swelling breasts of a young woman ; the *lacrimae* of 17 are drops of dew, they are also the tears of the virgin who must surrender to her husband ; in 19 *pudorem* describes the tip of the folded blossom, finally visible, but it also suggests the blushing modesty of a virgin bride. The roses are finally revealed, in 22, as naked maidens awaiting the mysteries of marriage.

We have already encountered the virgin's customary tears at the prospect of marital experience, but in the closing lines of the stanza the poet anticipates her freely-given surrender to the service of love. This is not apparently prompted by any fear of fading beauty, but is a willing response to the workings of the goddess. The initiation which represents its climax is no longer seen as a ritual of submission, but as an act of dedication ; and the plucking of the rose, the focal point of other treatments of the motif, is unmentioned ; symbolic development culminates, not in an act of plunder, but in maturity and self-revelation : the unfolding of the rose. The rose's traditional symbolism has been reinterpreted ; formerly a brittle symbol of transience and fragility and of a vulnerable innocence which is lost in a ritual of violent assertion and submission, it has become the metaphor through which the poet suggests the development of maturing womanhood. The consummation of this process is not presented, through the symbol of plucking the rose, as a ceremony of loss or deprivation, but, through the image of its unfolding, as a sacrament of self-expression and fulfilment.

The description of the growth and opening of rose blooms in this stanza of the *Pervigilium*, which at the same time evokes the physical and emotional evolution of a young woman, is one of the minor miracles of Latin literature.

13. *ipsa* : referring, of course, to Venus ; cf. note on *ipsa* in 63.
gemmis floridis : Rigler's correction for *gemmis ... floribus* in the MSS which is preserved by Cazzaniga and gives a possible meaning : *ipsa annum, gemmis purpurantem, pingit floribus* : she herself adorns with flowers the year which is (already) aglow with buds. But considerations of both thought and style commend Rigler's simple emendation. Throughout this stanza each repetition of *ipsa* seems to introduce a new development in the wonderful process by which Venus unfolds and awakens the roses. The first line of the stanza should therefore evoke the first stage of the miracle, describing how the goddess decorates the spring landscape with flower-buds, while the appearance of the flowers themselves, the *flores*, is

only anticipated later in 20-26. Moreover the poet's description of the roses is non-literal throughout ; the buds are swelling breasts (14), enwrapped by a dripping robe (21) ; they are *florulentae purpurae* (19) and even when openly called *rosae* (22) they are more besides : they are *virgines*. In this context, where the style is at once delightfully periphrastic and charged with metaphorical suggestion, *gemmis floridis* is far more appropriate than the prosaic reading of the MSS. Clementi compares the expression here with Apul., *Met.* X, 29 : *solabar clades ultimas quod ver in ipso ortu iam gemmulis floridis cuncta depingeret et iam purpureo nitore prata vestiret.*

purpurantem : post-classical but used as early as Apuleius.

14. *papillas* : refers not to the whole buds, but to the folded blooms swelling within their sheaths ; these sheaths are the *umens peplum* which is to be laid aside on the morning of the festival.

15. *urget in nodos tepentes. Nodos* is the conjecture of a friend of Scriverius for *totos* (TV : *notos* S), while *tepentes* is Lipsius' suggestion for *pentes* (T : *penates* SV).

   Several editors (notably Wernsdorf, Buecheler, and Cazzaniga) have retained the reading of S. Wernsdorf writes : 'ego inhaerendum censeo Salmasianae lectioni, et *notos penates* interpretor corticem nascentis rosae, quem quasi domicilium suum magis magisque crescendo implet, usque dum pandat se et in calathum abeat, sicut cellas granorum in malo punico Avienus in carm. de mal. pun. *domos* vocavit. *Noti penates* sunt sui vel apti a natura dari'. But note the relevant lines of Avienus :

>   *tunc, ne pressa gravi sub pondere grana liquescant,*
>   *divisere domos.*
>
>   (Avieni Carm. ed. A. Holder, I, 18-19)

This does not convince me that our poet would write about *penates* of *papillae* ; the expression here, in S, in which the *papillae*, actual blooms and metaphorical breasts, are driven into and fill their *penates*, is unnatural and harsh, particularly on the metaphorical level which is elsewhere developed with great subtlety. Cazzaniga defends the reading of S by reference to *Georgic* IV, 153-5, where the hives of the bees are called *penates* :

>   *solae communes natos, consortia tecta*
>   *urbis habent, magnisque agitant sub legibus aevum,*
>   *et patriam solae et certos novere penates.*

But the description of bee-hives as *urbis, patriam* and finally *penates* by analogy with human society, especially in the context of *Georgic* IV, is far easier than its use to describe the sheaths which enfold the *papillae* of roses. The reading of S, in spite of the strictures of Clementi and Schilling, gives a *possible* meaning, but the expression represents a clumsy mixed metaphor, untypical and unworthy of the poet. It is this which convinces me of the need for emendation.

Nodos is certainly right, cf. *A.L.* 84, 7 : *dumque explicat altera nodum* (of a rose) ; *A.L.* 87, 3 : *nodo maiore tumentes* ; *A.L.* 253, 54 :

> *et roseis crinem nodis subnecte decenter.*

Tepentes is less certain but emerges on paleographical and literary considerations as the most satisfying of the many conjectures. It is not difficult to imagine how, through syllabic omission, *tepentes* might become *pentes* (T and A), in turn corrected to *penates* (S and V). *Tepens* is frequently used to describe the quickening west wind of spring (e.g. Virg., *Georg.* II, 330-1) or applied to spring itself (Ovid, *A.A.* III, 185-6). In the *Pervigilium* the epithet is transferred to the flowers themselves because of the metaphorical function of the stanza ; it describes the awakening desire of the maiden as well as the unfolding of roses. For *tepere* in this sense cf. Hor., *Carm.* I, 4, 19-20 :

> *nec tenerum Lycidan mirabere, quo calet iuventus*
> *nunc omnis et mox virgines tepebunt.*

It is because of this suggestive quality of *tepentes*, which evokes an emotional as well as a physical condition, that I prefer it to *tumentes* (Crusius and Schilling). *Patentes* (Ribbeck, also inserted in A) is paleographically easy but the rose-buds should not yet be opening, while the poet already dwells at enough length upon the colour of the roses (and the modesty of the virgins) without admission of Bouhier's *rubentes*.

The meaning of the whole phrase has been widely misunderstood by editors, cf. the translations of Mackail (1912), Clementi and Schilling, who all take *urgere in nodos tepentes* (*tumentes* Schilling) to mean that the *papillae* swell and partially unfold to become glowing, or swelling, clusters of buds. But the force of *urgere in* must represent movement into or against something and cannot describe transformation. The *papillae* are the folded blooms of the flowers themselves, the *nodi* are the buds or sheaths which enfold them as an *umens peplum*. Lines 13-21 describe three main stages in the unfolding of the roses ; in 14-15 Dione drives (*urget in*) the swelling blooms into their protective sheaths ; this is growth inside the buds ; these are then loosened by dew (15-19) so that the red tip of the flowers within becomes visible ; this has already happened (*prodiderunt*, 19). The third stage is anticipated in 20-21, where the poet describes how the dew, emphatically reintroduced as *umor ille*, will perform its final service and free the *virgineas papillas* from their moist garments. The roses will then be ready to obey the summons of the goddess and dedicate themselves to the service of love.

17. *emicant* : this, the emendation of Achilles Statius, is more vivid than Lipsius' *et micant* where *et* is flat and unnecessary. Schulzius' *en micant* is an improvement upon this, but the exclamatory *en* is best saved for 19 alone where it thus concentrates our attention upon the sudden trans-formation of the roses.

18. This is one of the least happy lines in the poem, amounting to little more than a prosaic reformulation of the idea so imaginatively expressed in the previous line. *Praeceps* here does not describe swift or violent motion, but downward tendency. The poet is thinking of the pear-shaped dewdrops which hang from the tips of leaves or flowers in apparent defiance of the laws of gravity.
sustinet : here means to 'check', 'restrain'.

19. *en* ! Bouhier's certain correction of the MSS reading *in*, which does not make sense. In my note to line 15 I pointed to the perfect tense *prodiderunt* : the action of the line has already taken place. *En* qualifies the tense of the verb, which describes something which has just taken place before the eyes of the poet himself. The tip of the rose-bloom has become visible, the maiden has blushed at the thought of what tomorrow brings !

19-20. These lines, as previous editors have realised, are imitated by Fulgentius, cf. Mit. I, 11 :

> *ubi guttas florulentae mane rorant purpurae,*
> *umor algens quem serenis astra sudant noctibus.*

21. *Mane ... solvit. Mane* could be referred to past time and *solvit* construed as a perfect tense, but the emphatic designation *umor ille* seems to announce further development rather than recapitulation, and the repetition of *mane* in 22, where it must mean 'tomorrow morning', retrospectively invites a similar interpretation of the earlier usage. I therefore take *solvit* as *praesens pro futuro* ; cf. my comments on *dicit* in line 7 and 51.

The employment of *mane* referring to tomorrow morning is no nearer the Italian *domani*, as Clementi has claimed, than standard classical usage ; cf. Cic., *Tusc.* V, 121 : *sed quoniam mane est eundum, has quinque dierum disputationes memoria comprehendamus* ; Ovid, *Am.* I, 6, 69-70 (he is addressing the coronal which he is leaving on his mistress' doorstep) :

> *tu dominae, cum te proiectam mane videbit,*
> *temporis absumpti tam male testis erit.*

21. *virgineas papillas.* This is the reading of S, T and A. Lipsius, presumably to avoid the dactyl in the second foot, conjectured *virgines* without knowledge of V. But second-foot dactyls also occur in lines 17 and 87, while the adjective *virgineus* is appropriately used to describe a part of the roses, the substantive *virgines* being reserved for the whole blooms in 22.
    umenti peplo. This dripping garment is the sheath, the dull sepals which form the outer cover of the bud before it opens. *Peplum* is, in classical Latin, used specifically of a ritual garment offered to Minerva (cf. Virg., *Aen.* I, 480 ; Stat., *Theb.* X, 56), but later poets extend the usage to embrace any splendid garment (cf. Claud., *De Nupt. Hon.* 122) and Ausonius uses the word metaphorically (*Mos.* 419). For the idea here in the *P.V.*, cf. *A.L.* 84, 8 (quoted by Schilling) :

> *ac dum virgineus pudor exsinuatur amictu* (of a rose-bloom)

22. *nudae virgines nubant rosae. Nudae* is Mackail's correction of the MSS, although the reading of V (and S, when the simple dittographical error has been eliminated) gives a possible meaning ; the adverb *tute* might be used to emphasise the nature of Venus' activity in the *Pervigilium*, where she is not the fickle goddess of the elegists but the patroness of secure love-union, *amorum copulatrix.* Trotski (1926) quotes line 82, where *tutus* evokes the peaceful stability which the poet imagines to be a quality of love amongst animals, in defence of the MSS reading here, but the analogy is hardly conclusive. *Tute*, as an alternative for *tuto*, is very rare, although *tutae*, Scaliger's correction of *tuae* in T, is not subject to this objection ; but the phrase *tutae virgines* inevitably suggests that their coming marriage will never be consummated ! Moreover both readings give a rather forced and intrusively abstract emphasis in a stanza where the description throughout is both visually and metaphorically satisfying. We need a term which applies with equal felicity to both roses and maidens.

Clementi and Schilling adopt the conjecture made independently by both Dousa maior and Achilles Statius : *mane ut udae*. But although *udae* is a happy usage with *rosae*, meaning dew-drenched roses, the metaphorical interpretation which the phrase *udae virgines* compels (cf. Martial, XI, 16, 8) conveys a notion of concupiscence which is foreign to the emotional context of the stanza, where the awakening desire of the virgin is suggested with great delicacy. Orelli's *totae* is equally out of place in lines so remarkable for imaginative expression.

The clue to the true reading is to be found in line 21 where the poet describes how the dew will free the virginal breasts from the garment which has covered them. The roses will then be ready, as *nudae virgines*, naked virgins, to obey the summons of the goddess and offer themselves to love. Paleographical justification for this conjecture is at hand in line 15 where *nodos* has become *notos* in S and *totos* in T and V. By a similar process of confusion *nudae* has resulted in *tute*.

23. *Cypridis* : for the MSS reading *prius*. The context clearly demands a proper name. Schilling instances *A.L.* 85 in support of *Cypridis* :

> *aut hoc risit Amor, aut hoc de pectine traxit*
> *purpureis Aurora comis, aut sentibus haesit*
> *Cypris et hic spinis insedit sanguis acutis.*

Clementi conjectured *Paphies*, but the alliteration of the phrase *facta Cypridis de cruore* seems typical of our poet. *Cypridis* has become *pridis* through omission of the first syllable under the influence of the prevailing rhythm ; this, in turn, has been 'corrected' to *prius*.

Cazzaniga reads *patrio de cruore* (Hermann, in his ed., proposes *patris*), and refers lines 23-6, not to the marriage of the roses, but to the birth of Venus and her *hieros gamos* with Anchises, which, he claims, the festival as a whole celebrates (cf. Cazzaniga, 63-75 ; *id., 'Il Pervigilium Veneris'*, *Nuova Antologia* Nov. 1956, 331-42 ; also E. Griset, *RSC* V (1957) 169-74). This proposal is so fundamental that it is worth considering in detail why it is impossible :

a) In order to force line 22 into a meaning consistent with his version of 23-6, Cazzaniga interprets *nubant* metaphorically and takes *virgines* as its object : the goddess has ordered the roses to marry maidens (which means that the virgin attendants of the goddess will be garlanded with roses when they celebrate the *Pervigilium*). Such a mode of expression is fanciful to the point of absurdity and *nubant* with an accusative is virtually unparalleled. Moreover that the poet is thinking of the roses as maidens has been clear from *papillas* in line 14 : *virgines* and *rosae* clearly belong together as complimentary nominatives.

b) The poet has already described Venus' birth ; to do so again, in an inconsistent, and far less impressive, manner, seems like an unnecessary indulgence.

c) To regard Eros as having any part in the birth of Venus is completely at variance with his presentation elsewhere in the *Pervigilium*, where he is specifically referred to as the child of Venus (77, cf. also 55) and, as the frivolous love-boy of Hellenistic tradition, preserves no traces of the primeval spirit of Hesiodic theogony.

d) The notion that roses sprang from the blood of Venus (*facta Cypridis de cruore*) is common in late Latin poetry ; cf. *A.L.* 85 quoted above ; *A.L.* 366, 4 ; Dracontius, *de origine rosarum*, 1-6 :

> *icitur alma Venus, dum Martis vitat amores*
> *et pedibus nudis florea prata premit :*
> *sacrilega placidas irrepsit spina per herbas*
> *et tenero plantas vulnere mox lacerat.*
> *funditur inde cruor, vestitur spina rubore ;*
> *quae scelus admisit, munus odoris habet.*

e) The description in 24 obviously refers to the roses, since *deque gemmis* picks up the earlier phrase *gemmis floridis* and *solis purpuris* echoes *florulentae purpurae* in 19.

Lines 23-6 definitely describe the origin and anticipate the marriage of roses. The singular participle following the plural *virgines rosae* is no problem, especially as the poet employs the same technique of concentration in 17-18 where the *lacrimae trementes* become the singular *gutta praeceps*.

25. *ruborem* : the crimson centre of the rose-blossom, the virginity of the maiden which will tomorrow be surrendered.

veste ignea : perhaps an oblique reference to the *flammeum*, the Roman bridal veil, and distinct, I think, from the *umens peplum* of 21 which (cf. note *ad loc.*), describing the dull-green sheath of the bud, does not qualify for the epithet *igneum*. The flower-petals themselves are the *vestis ignea* which shield the scarlet eye of the bloom and will unfold tomorrow to reveal the *ruborem* within.

26. *unico marita nodo*. Almost all modern editors (Baehrens, Owen, Rand, Clementi, Schilling and Cazzaniga) adopt Bergk's emendation (*unico*

marita voto) of the obviously corrupt MSS, but I suspect that *voto*, carrying the post-classical sense of a marriage vow, represents a case of improving our poet rather than restoring his text. For *nodo*, the reading of V and T, gives a perfectly good sense with the simple emendation *unico*, and it is perhaps significant that S, which reads *noto* here, also preserves *notos* for the certain *nodos* at line 15.

Pithou, reading *unico nodo*, referred the phrase to the knot of the bride's girdle, loosed to the embraces of her husband, but this gives no satisfactory meaning to *unico*. Wernsdorf, followed by Mackail, conjectured *uvido nodo* − 'the nuptial rose will not be ashamed to unfold her crimson from the moist bud' − but although this gives an excellent meaning and may be right, I feel that the metaphor which has been sustained and developed throughout the stanza, is finally emerging into dominance and that, with *marita*, the conceptual emphasis of *unicus*, explaining that the bride will remain faithful to a single lover, is here to be preferred to the purely descriptive force of *uvidus*. For this usage of *unicus* Clementi instances Hor., *Carm.* III, 14, 5 :

> *unico gaudens mulier marito.*

And Schilling compares the idea here with Prop. IV, 11, 36 :

> *in lapide hoc uni nupta fuisse legar.*

Moreover the proud claim which Propertius attributes to Cornelia is also encountered on many Roman epitaphs ; cf. Buecheler, *Carm. Ep. Lat.* I, 548, 553, 558, 560, and elsewhere.

Nodus is to be interpreted metaphorically ; previously used to describe swelling buds it now represents the physical and emotional ties of sexual union. For *nodus* of sexual involvement cf. Lucr., IV, 1147-8 ; for spiritual affection cf. Cic., *De Am.* XIV, 51.

The reading *unico nodo* thus gives an excellent sense : the maiden is to dedicate herself in devoted and faithful union. This is the nature of the love which Venus inspires.

I can see a possible objection to this interpretation in the progression *ruborem ... nodo ... solvere. Nodo* is perhaps most easily understood as an ablative of place, as the bud from which the rose will unfold the crimson of her bloom, rather than as a descriptive ablative with *marita*. If this consideration is felt to be convincing Wernsdorf's *uvido* must be substituted for *unico*.

Buecheler understood the reading of S (*noto*) as a proper name, the ablative of *Notus*, the South Wind : the rose will unfold her crimson to the caress of the South Wind. This is a charming idea, but the metre demands rearrangement (*Noto marita*) and the sense requires emendation (*uvido* for *unico*) ; I do not think so fanciful a notion justifies these changes.

26. *pudebit* : this personal usage of *pudeo* is archaic and very rare, cf. *Lex. Tot. Lat. ad loc.*

solvere : the rose unfolds the heart of the bloom, the maiden 'unties' her virginity, a highly effective metonymy evoking the naked and blushing surrender of the young bride. Catullus expresses the same idea less imaginatively in LXI, 52-3 :

> *tibi virgines*
> *zonula solvunt sinus.*

STANZA IV : VENUS AND CUPID

We now come to the poet's description of the festival itself. The significance of the festival-motif and the rôle of the nymphs within its ritual is discussed elsewhere, cf. 'the Festival', pp. 25-33 ; my concern here is with the presence of Cupid, and with Venus' warning to beware him.

In Roman literature Cupid generally acts either as the servant of Venus (cf. *Aen.* I, 657-756), or mother and son work in partnership. Hence throughout elegiac poetry the terms *Venus, Amor* and *Cupido* are used as virtual synonyms. But Cupid makes no appearance in the Catullan *epithalamium Manlii et Iuniae*, where Venus depends upon the good offices of Hymen :

> *dux bonae Veneris, boni*
> *coniugator amoris.*   (44-5)

Indeed the moral quality of love depends upon the favour of Hymen, not of Venus :

> *nil potest sine te Venus,*
> *fama quod bona comprobet,*
> *commodi capere, at potest*
> *te volente.*   (61-4)

Beyond the context of marriage Venus does not act as a moral agent but, by implication, as the Venus of adultery and passion. This the poet of the *Pervigilium* would never admit, nor would he allow the beneficence of her influence to depend upon the cooperation of another god. But even

Catullus' insistence upon the benevolence of Venus in her epithalamic rôle is not clearly maintained in the later tradition, where Cupid significantly acts as her chief assistant.

Thus in Statius' *epithalamium* (*Silv.* I, 2) Cupid appears as his mother's principal agent, mischievously inspiring the love which she is later to sanction. Throughout this poem love is described, in conventional elegiac terms, as excruciating pain. The more it hurts, the better Cupid and Venus are pleased. Note too Statius' description of Venus and her attendants :

> *forte, serenati qua stat plaga lactea caeli,*
> *alma Venus thalamo pulsa modo nocte iacebat*
> *amplexu duro Getici resoluta mariti.*
> *fulcra torosque deae tenerum premit agmen Amorum.*
> *signa petunt quas ferre faces, quae pectora figi*
> *imperet ; an terris saevire an malit in undis,*
> *an miscere deos an adhuc vexare Tonantem.*
> *ipsi animus nondum nec cordi fixa voluntas.*
> *fessa iacet stratis, ubi quondam conscia culpae*
> *Lemnia deprenso repserunt vincula lecto.*　　　　　　　　(51-60)

Here, in the context of an *epithalamium*, Statius playfully refers to Venus' adultery with Mars and the scandal of its exposure. She is surrounded by a troop of *Amores*, awaiting her instructions to inflame and transfix her chosen victims. Will she rage over the earth or the sea ? Will she concentrate her malice upon Jupiter ? These are the considerations which absorb the languid adulteress who is so soon to preside over the nuptials of Stella and Violentilla !

The later poet Claudian, in his *Epithalamium Honorii*, again makes Cupid the prime-mover of love. Venus is delighted by his malignant warfare (109-16) and recalls with amusement to what humiliating lengths he has driven even Jupiter. Claudian also describes the Cyprian paradise of Venus (49-90) ; it is inhabited by a squadron of *Amores*, and by various personified aspects of love (77-85), by Licence, Anger, Tears and Perjury. Such are the attendants of the goddess who is shortly to unite Honorius and Maria in marriage !

So far we have seen Cupid presented as his mother's senior lieutenant ; but, although not an *epithalamium*, we find a poem of Dracontius (*Rom.* II) in which Venus, while begging Cupid's assistance in an act of revenge, confesses herself to be his virtual inferior (cf. 46-51), and is portrayed as effectively impotent without the support of her son.

Dracontius probably wrote after the poet of the *Pervigilium* and Claudian may also be later, but similar presentations of Venus, even in the epithalamic tradition, as a frivolous libertine, who indulgently admires, sanctions and even depends upon the malevolent sport of her son, must have been composed at all periods of the Empire. The treatment of Venus and Cupid, in later *epithalamia*, preserves no vestige of religious feeling ; they are purely literary figures who provide a suitable excuse for the frivolous elaboration of conventional tropes.

The *Pervigilium Veneris* is, also, in a sense, an *epithalamium*, but it is the wedding-song of all creation and Venus is very much more than a creature of literary fancy ; she is the mother of creation and the moral inspiration of the universe. As such she cannot preserve her working partnership with Cupid and therefore explicitly orders the nymphs to beware him ; nor can she appear as the mistress of Mars and the goddess, not only of marital union, but of elegiac passion. Either association would conflict with the poet's celebration of her as the source and patron of cosmic harmony.

It is, I think, to dissociate his Venus from the traditional Venus of Roman literature that the poet now introduces Cupid, not as her servant and ally, but as a potential threat to the security of love which the festival celebrates. The technique is one of implicit contrast. The harmonious union which Venus promotes is opposed to the activity of the frivolous love-boy who, with his bow, arrows and torch, represents the habitual torments of elegiac love. Indeed the agonies which his paraphernalia symbolise are seen to be of his very essence, for, although stripped of his weapons and naked, Cupid is beautiful ; wherefore :

> *totus est in armis idem quando nudus est Amor.*

This stanza, with its description of the ritual procession to the sanctuary of the goddess, is primarily decorative and lighthearted, but the poet seizes upon the presence of Cupid as a means of emphasizing, by contrast, the moral seriousness of his conception of Venus.

28. *luco ... myrteo* ; dative after verb of motion, found in Augustan poetry ; e.g. Virg., *Aen*. V, 451.

29. *it* : Pithou's certain correction of *et* (STV).
    comes : the reading of S ; Valgiglio's fatuous defence of *comis* (TV) will convince no-one with any feeling for style.

31. Note the tribrach in the third foot.

32. *nudus ire iussus est*. Love, in his deceptive simplicity, is commonly imagined to be naked ; cf. Prop., I, 2, 8 ; Ov., *Am*. I, 10, 15-16. For the idea of the unarming of *Amor*, cf. Tib., II, 5, 105-6.

33. *neu ... neu ... neu*. The first *neu* of this series, which thus introduces a negative purpose, while the remainder quite regularly supply supplementary notions, is parallelled by *neve ... neve* at Prop., II, 29, 28. The reason for this very rare usage is the poet's fondness for repetition as a feature of structure at the beginning of each full metron, cf. 24, 54, 65.

35. *totus est in armis*. Pithou's emendation, *in armis* for *inermis*, is certainly right. Retention of *inermis* compels the following translation of 34-5 : 'but, nymphs, beware, for Love is beautiful ; he is quite harmless when he is naked'. This is nonsense, whereas Pithou's correction gives exactly the sense demanded by the context. *Amor's* power is seen to reside, not in his weapons, but in himself, in his beauty, hence the paradox that Love is most dangerous precisely when he is naked and defenceless.

To avoid the third-foot spondee which this emendation introduces, Saumaise altered the word-order of the line : *est in armis totus idem*. Cf. metrical discussion, pp. 34-9.

totus. Clementi follows Fort in considering this usage 'probably colloquial'. But the adverbial use of the nominative adjective *totus* is common in classical poetry and the best prose. Cf. Caes., *B.G.* VI, 5 ; Cic., *Clu*. XXVI, 72 ; Hor., *Sat*. I, 9, 2.

STANZA V : VENUS AND DIANA

Venus now sends a chorus of virgins to command the withdrawal of Diana, the virgin huntress, from her forest glades. The goddess of love is to supplant the virgin as queen of the woods. For Diana's traditional significance as mistress of the woodlands, cf. Cat. XXXIV, 9-12.

The development of the stanza reveals the central feature of the *Pervigilium* as a ritual of initiation, for, while the virgin Diana must depart, the choir of virgins obviously remain as devotees of Venus. The reason is made clear in 40-1, where the virgins explain that if Venus could influence Delia, if the chaste huntress would submit to love, then she would gladly be welcomed amongst the devotees of the *Pervigilium*. It is her unyielding insistence upon her virginity which makes this impossible. The only inference which can reasonably be drawn from such a statement

is that the nymphs will do what the Delian refuses to do and surrender to
the experience of love :

   regnet in silvis Dione, tu recede Delia.

The poet's emphasis upon the innocence of his nymphs is another
reminder that Venus does not inspire the concupiscence of elegiac frenzy,
but the evolution of that tender susceptibility which was described metaphorically in stanza III.

37-38. Riese indicates a lacuna after 36, believing a line *cum Dianae com-*
memoratione to have been lost. He has not been followed by subsequent
editors, in spite of the following difficulties :

   1) *conpari pudore* : this phrase seems strangely adrift at the beginning
of the stanza. Does it describe *Venus* or *virgines*, and who is the object of
comparison ? It is true that the context helps us to puzzle out these
problems, but the awkwardness remains, for the word-order suggests that
pudore be taken with Venus, while the sense demands that it should be
referred to *virgines* (cf. below).
   2) *ad te*. We must wait for the vocative in 38 for this abrupt personal
address to be made clear, and for the force of *conpari* finally to emerge.
   3) *rogamus* : an unannounced transition into direct speech. Doubtless
due to the rudimentary nature of their punctuation, Roman narrative and
lyric poets usually introduce speech or dialogue in as unambiguous a
manner as possible. Is line 37 part of the virgin's valediction to Diana, or
does it represent the poet's introduction of the chorus of maidens ?
   The collective force of these problems of transition persuades me to
adopt Riese's lacuna. Note, too, the poet's method in the surrounding
stanzas, both of which begin with an emphatic command by the goddess
herself, while the further course of each stanza expands and develops this
initial summons. Rather than the single line suggested by Riese, I suspect
that several lines have been lost, lines in which Venus, probably
introduced as *ipsa* or *ipsa diva*, commanded the nymphs to approach
Diana, the virgin goddess, and to order her departure from the forest.
These lines would have provided an antecedent for *ad te*, would have
clarified the comparative function of *conpari pudore*, and would have
introduced the speech of the virgins which, beginning with what is now
line 37, occupies the remainder of the stanza.
   Doubtless the MSS line-order can be retained by defending the abrupt
beginning of the strophe as a deliberate technique which avoids

unnecessary description by leaving the reader to supply transitional detail. This is an argument unworthy of our poet who, I feel convinced, never intended to lead us into this stanza with such an ungainly lurch.

conpari pudore. Clementi refers the phrase to Venus and translates, or rather paraphrases : 'with her own shy blushes Venus sendeth unto thee her maids'. But the theme of the stanza demands that *conpari pudore* should be construed with *virgines*, and the Venus of the *Pervigilium* is neither shy nor bashful. As virgins the nymphs share the virginal modesty of Diana, a quality which they will however surrender together with their virginity (cf. stanza III), while the implacably chaste Diana must withdraw and leave the forest free for love. This has been misunderstood by Ussani who conjectured *non pari pudore*.

40. I follow the anonymous Leipzig editor of 1872 in transposing line 58, which is clearly dislocated, to become line 40 of my text. This transposition is accepted by Buecheler, Mackail (1912), Rand (*TAPHA*, 1934) and Clementi, who all, however, together with the Leipzig editor, adopt Scaliger's *recentibus* in place of the MSS *rigentibus* ; but it is precisely *rigentibus*, meaning 'stiff', 'upright' (i.e. untrampled) which confirms the transposition and gives a more apposite meaning in context than the arguably more poetic, but certainly less appropriate, *recentibus*. For a comparable usage, cf. Tiberianus, I, 11 :

> *roscidum nemus rigebat inter uda gramina.*

Retention of the MSS reading disposes of Schilling's objections to this transposition (notes to 58) and precludes consideration of the alternative solutions of Riese, who (reading *ut* for *et*) inserts the line to follow 52, and Martin (1935) who, with *ducit* for *ducat*, places 58-62 after line 7. Trotski, Schilling and Cazzaniga all reject transposition and indicate a lacuna around 58, but the subjunctive *ducat* together with the supremely appropriate *rigentibus* both proclaim the true home of this displaced line.

40. *te rogare*. Saumaise's simple correction of the MSS *erogare*, which does not make sense. T and A both omit this line. The use of the imperfect subjunctive of *volo*, to express a wish dependent upon an impossible condition, is standard Latinity.

42. *feriatis noctibus*. Presumably objecting to the use of the participial adjective *feriatis* with an impersonal noun, Scriverius (*feriantis*) and Pithou (*feriatos*) both emend to gain agreement with *choros*. Pithou's *feriatos* is far preferable (use of the present participle is very rare) and

perhaps gives a more pleasing adjectival balance than the MSS reading, but neither emendation is justified as the use of *feriatus* to qualify an inanimate object, though uncommon, is well-attested (cf. *Thes.* s.v.).

43. *congreges* : a post-classical word, but found as early as Apuleius, cf. *Thes.* s.v.

45. The festival is attended by Bacchus, Ceres and Apollo (*poetarum deus*), by Cupid, the Graces and by nymphs. The last three appear as Venus' entourage in Hor., *Carm.* I, 30, 1-6. For nymphs and Graces in the goddess' retinue, cf. *id.*, I, 4, 5-7 ; IV, 7, 5-6. As gods of plenty and mirth, Ceres and Bacchus are summoned to the rustic festival in Tibullus, II, 1, 3-4 :

> *Bacche, veni, dulcisque tuis e cornibus uva*
> *pendeat, et spicis tempora cinge, Ceres.*

cf. also Tib., III, 7, 163. The presence of these gods and demi-gods in the *Pervigilium* is thus explicable in terms of a literary, rather than a local religious, tradition, while the poet himself indicates his reasons for Apollo's attendance ; cf. further my discussion of the festival, pp. 31-5.

46. *detinenda ... pervigilanda*. S seems to indicate the original presence of two gerundives, restored by Heinsius as *detinenda* and *perviglanda*. *Detinenda* does not need defending against Cazzaniga's ridiculous *continenter* and from where have Schenkl and Baehrens conjured *detinenter* ? Owen suggests *pervigilia* in place of *perviglanda*, but he can only support this feminine form of the adjective *pervigil* from the Justinianus, while our poet only once elsewhere employs a tribrach (and there after a spondee, 31). Moreover the balance of the two gerundives is intrinsically appealing. If the contracted form of the second gerundive is felt to be objectionable, should we not consider the claims of the full form ? Clementi's Horatian analogies in favour of syncopation prove nothing beyond the permissibility of syncope in Latin poetry, which is scarcely in doubt ; nor do I see anything fundamentally impossible in the pre-tonic contraction which *perviglanda* introduces into the text. The *Appendix Probi* (Keil IV, 193-204) provides further examples of syncope after the plosive 'g' (for no-one, I imagine, would foist the orthography of S upon our poet here), although the *Appendix* is citing, and correcting, vulgar practice. But note how both V and T seem to have corrupted the full form of the gerundive. Presuming, therefore, that their MSS forbears once preserved *pervigilanda*, it appears more likely that the scribe of S, perhaps misled by the

prevailing rhythm of the metre, or by his own Latinity, should have unconsciously introduced a syncopation, than that a copyist should have been so disturbed by this syncopation as to substitute the full form along with a fifth-foot dactyl. But there can, of course, be no objection to a dactyl here, as the anapaests at 55 and 62, and spondees at 50, 60 and 91, prove that the poet did not regard a pure trochee as compulsory in this position. Moreover he is generally fonder of dactylic than of anapaestic resolution. Weighing the balance of probabilities I have therefore cautiously restore the uncontracted form of the gerundive, *pervigilanda*.

STANZA VI : HYBLA

For the significance of the Hyblaean setting of the *P.V.* cf. 'the Festival' pp. 30-4.

tribunal. Cf. the *thronus sublimis* in line 7. The metaphor is now drawn from a court-of-law rather than an imperial council, for Dione is to publish her edicts from the raised platform upon which Roman magistrates sat in judgment. This is, to my knowledge, the first specific reference to a 'court of love' in Latin poetry.

50. *praeses* : Scaliger's correction for *praesens* in the MSS ; cf. 'the Metre', p. 38.

dicit, adsederunt. J. Dousa filius rejected the reading of the MSS and substituted *dicet, adsidebunt.* Clementi believed that these emendations were 'certainly correct' and commented, 'apart from the confusion of tenses in the MSS, a spondee in the fifth-foot is not permissible'.

The metrical argument is based on a false assumption, cf. my discussion of the metre pp. 35-8, while the 'confusion of tenses', to which Clementi refers, is a deliberate technique. The phrase *iura dicit* is repeated from line 6 and is an obvious instance of *praesens pro futuro*, a usage found also in line 45 :

nec Ceres nec Bacchus absunt nec poetarum deus.

The present tense used of future time becomes increasingly common in Late Latin (cf. Leum., II, 307-8) and is a dramatic feature of the *Pervigilium*, contributing to the sense of excitement and expectation which pervades the poem. The meaning, and appropriateness, of the perfect *adsederunt* is also clear ; the Graces have *already* taken their seats and are awaiting the arrival of their mistress. This again reinforces the tense and expectant air in which the beginning of the festival is awaited. The use of *dicit, adsederunt* is thus not an example of confusion of tenses, but rather of their imaginative use ; now that the metrical fallacy upon which emendation rests has been exploded, the reading of the MSS can be confidently retained as in every way preferable to Lipsius' less vivid future tenses ; cf. particularly 'the Metre', p. 41.

51. *totos*. Already in classical Latin *totus* can be used with the force of *omnis* (cf. *Thes.* s.v.) but this becomes increasingly common in later Latin (cf. Leum., II, 203).
quidquid. The relative of the neuter singular *quidquid* after a masculine plural antecedent is not good Latin, and the analogies which Clementi cites (*ad loc.*) are substantival rather than relative ; we must understand a dependent genitive − *Hybla totos funde flores, quidquid (florum) annus adtulit*.

52. *florum sume vestem* : the emendation of Heinsius (1665). The MSS are clearly corrupt. S (*supe restem*) does not make sense, while the reading of V (*rumpe restem*) has the ring of a copyist's improvement upon the tradition preserved in T (*rumpe reste*) : it is an untypically harsh expression and I doubt whether *restis* can be used of a garland of flowers. Heinsius' correction is close to the reading of S and gives an excellent, and entirely appropriate, meaning. For both these reasons it is preferable to Scriverius' more fanciful *subde messem*.
Aetnae : the witness of V, probably a scribal emendation as the related errors in S (*et nec*) and T (*ethne*) suggest corruption at a very early stage before the stemma had split. Lipsius, without knowledge of V, conjectured *Ennae* (better spelt *Hennae*), but S and T both point to *Aetna* and the plain of Aetna was famous for its fertility (cf. Cic. *Verr.* II, 3, 18, cited by Clementi ; Claudian, *De Rapt. Pros.* II, 72 : *Aetna parens florum*). There is no reason to reject the reading in V. The reference here might be to the celebrated volcano and the plain beneath it, or to the ancient township called Aetna, situated at the foot of the mountain on the plain itself.

53. *vel* : even in classical Latin the disjunctive force of *vel* sometimes disappears, cf. Clementi *ad loc*.

54. *quaeque fontes incolunt*. The poet has already mentioned nymphs of the mountains in the preceding line. Repetition here would not be emphatic but merely redundant. As Schilling comments in his *apparatus* the MSS reading *montes* probably owes its existence to *montium* in 53 ; *fontes* is the

correction of Scriverius. Valgiglio (p. 129) prefers to read Sannazaro's marginal emendation *fontium* in 53, preserving *montes* here in 54. This is not impossible, but on the whole I prefer the broad distinction between *ruris* and *montium*, between nymphs of the lowlands and the wild mountains, while in the following line the poet associates the nymphs with more specific locales found in both types of landscape, with forest, grove and fountain.

55. *pueri mater alitis* : fifth-foot anapaest.

STANZA VII : THE MARRIAGE OF EARTH AND SKY

From the fantasy of the festival we now return to the realm of cosmic forces ; previously stated motifs are redeveloped and amplified. Line 2 declared *vere natus orbis est* ; this is now interpreted as a consequence of the primal marriage of earth and sky ; the *maritus imber* no longer, as in line 4, wakes only the forest to life, but, falling into the lap of mother earth, becomes the father of all things.

Among Roman poets both Lucretius and Virgil treat the *hieros gamos* of earth and sky (cf. Lucr., I, 248-53 ; II, 992-7 ; Virg., *Georg.*, II, 323-7), with the vital difference that neither poet uses the motif, like the poet of the *Pervigilium*, to express religious conviction or a metaphysical interpretation of nature. Lucretius turns to it as a vivid metaphor to illustrate the effects of atomic disruption and union, while Virgil creates a vivid and memorable personification of a natural process.

Statius' use of the topos is visually unexciting (cf. *Silv.* I, 2, 183-7) but, as in the *Pervigilium*, the *hieros gamos* is an expression of the cosmic power of Venus. The possible impact of the image is, however, destroyed by the fatuous context in which it finds itself, as the self-congratulatory assertion of a Venus who is no more than a creature of stale-literary fancy.

In this stanza of the *Pervigilium* the primeval union of earth and sky regains its former grandeur as the mythical expression of a divine presence within the events of nature. The language is Virgilian, but the feeling of the passage, as an expression of the cosmic power of love, is far closer to Aeschylus :

> ἐρᾷ μὲν ἁγνὸς οὐρανὸς τρῶσαι χθόνα,
> ἔρως δὲ γαῖαν λαμβάνει γάμου τυχεῖν,
> ὄμβρος δ᾽ ἀπ᾽ εὐνασθέντος οὐρανοῦ πεσὼν

ἔχυσε γαῖαν. ἢ δὲ τίχτεται βροτοῖς
μήλων τε βοσκὰς καὶ βίον Δημήτριον.
δενδρῶτις ὥρα δ'ἐκ νοτίζοντος γάμου
τέλειός ἐστι. τῶνδ' ἐγὼ παραίτιος .

(Frag. *Danaids*, Athenaeus XIII, 600b)

Aphrodite is speaking. Note how she explains her influence with beguiling simplicity : τῶνδ' ἐγὼ παραίτιος , whereas in the *Pervigilium* mythical statement is enriched by the poet's philosophical development of the concept of *Venus procreatrix*, the cosmic mother who rules the inner world of creation with her all-pervasive spirit. Important, too, is the verb *gubernat*, which is not a verb of power only but of quality, evoking the secure and ordered dominion of the divine *procreatrix*.

'In this passage', writes Clementi, 'the Stoic *anima mundi* is identified with Venus', and both Trotski and Schilling emphasise the Stoical colour of the stanza. But although one or two phrases may ultimately derive from Stoic concepts (notably *pervius tenor*, cf. notes on 63, 64, 66 below), the language, I think, is drawn from the philosophical κοινή of late antiquity and the fundamental ideas, of God and nature, are not Stoical. For Stoic theology is essentially pantheistic ; traditional anthropomorphism is allegorised into philosophical abstracts, and these abstract notions of spirit, soul and creative fire (*ignis artificiosa*) are wholly identified with the universe they animate (cf. Seneca, *Nat. Quaest.* II, 45, and Cicero's exposition of the views of Zeno, *De Nat. Deorum*, XXII, 57-8). But the Venus of the *Pervigilium* is not an allegorical conception ; she is the *procreatrix*, endowed with a life and personality which exist apart from her creation ; and nor is her nature submerged in either her *permeans spiritus* or her *pervius tenor* (unlike Clementi, Schilling, *intro*. p. L, has realised this) ; these are divine attributes not theological absolutes.

Schilling, moreover, is wrong to insist that fire is, for the poet of the *Pervigilium*, an essential constituent of the creative process. There is no evidence for this anywhere in the poem, where the constant emphasis is upon the generative power of the celestial *umor*, whether as dew, as the *maritus imber* or as *cruor supernus*. The poet's account of the birth of Venus betrays none of the allegorising tendencies noted by Schilling in Varro's explanation of the myth (*De Ling. Lat.* V, 63, Schilling XLIX-L) and it is a simple misrepresentation to imply that *cruor supernus* represents a virtual synonym for *semen igneum*. The rose, it is true, is said (line 24) to have been made from, among other things, flames, but this evokes the crimson of its petals (cf. *A.L.* 366, 1-2) and does not express a philosophical conviction about the elements of matter.

The influence of Stoicism on the *Pervigilium Veneris* has been exaggerated. In this stanza of the poem the idea of divinity as a personal and beneficent spirit which governs, but exists apart from, the universe, is far nearer the god of the Hermetic Asclepius, or the ruling spirit of Apuleius' *De Mundo*, while, for the overall conception of Venus in the *Pervigilium*, we might perhaps compare Apuleius' portrayal of Isis in the last book of the *Metamorphoses* (particularly the wonderful invocation at XI, 25, 1-6).

59. *quo* : a temporal ablative equivalent to *quo tempore* or *quo die* (cf., for example, Ov., *Met.* I, 256-7) ; there is no reason for Buecheler's *quom*, an ante-classical spelling of *cum* still common in Cicero, but which, here in the *Pervigilium*, would represent an affected archaism for which there exists virtually no support elsewhere in the poem. *Pudebit*, in 26, hardly allows us to regard our poet as an archaizer.
copulavit nuptias : Clementi cites Digest. XII, 4, 6 : *copulare matrimonium* ; but closer to the wording here is Apul., *Met.* II, 12 : *qui dies copulas nuptiarum adfirmet.*

60. *totum ... annum* : Saumaise's correction for *totis* of the MSS gives a far more natural emphasis and a more pleasing adjectival balance in the line. For the phrase *totus annus* cf. Ov., *Fast.* I, 26 ; *ib.* I, 168, but *annus*, of course, is used by the poet of the *P.V.*, not with reference to the yearly succession of months and seasons, but to describe the annual cycle of growth and new life which begins in spring and culminates in harvest ; *totum annum* is an equivalent for *omnes anni fruges*, cf. Lucan, III, 70 :

> *effusis magnum Libye tulit imbribus annum.*

vernis : fifth-foot spondee.

61. *maritus imber* : that *maritus* here means 'husband' or 'conjugal' is confirmed by the nearby *coniugis*. Cf. notes on lines 4 and 11.

62. *fetus omnis.* The meaning of *fetus* is virtually synonymous with *annum* in 60 ; *omnis* is therefore further support for Saumaise's *totum*.
aleret : anapaestic fifth foot.

63. *ipsa*. Clementi objects that the MSS line-order requires that *ipsa* be referred to the preceding *almae coniugis*, Mother Earth, and transposes lines 63-67 to follow 11. But *ipsa* is used throughout the poem as an

emphatic affirmation of Venus' presence at every level of creation ; moreover in colloquial Latin the demonstrative pronoun *ipse* is sometimes used as a substantive with the force 'master' or 'mistress', cf. Cat. III, 6-7 (of Lesbia's sparrow) :

> *nam mellitus erat suamque norat*
> *ipsam tam bene quam puella matrem.*

There is no difficulty in taking *ipsa* here as a further allusion to Venus and consequently no justification for Clementi's transposition.
venas atque mentem. For *venas* cf. Virg., *Aen.* IV, 1-2 :

> *At regina gravi iamdudum saucia cura*
> *vulnus alit venis et caeco carpitur igni.*

Servius comments : *quia per venas amor currit ut sanguis ; nam in sanguine anima, in anima amor est.* Dido is both bodily and emotionally possessed by her passion. Similarly I do not think that *venas* in the *Pervigilium* represents merely 'flesh' (Mackail) as opposed to the spirit, and nor is its use purely metaphorical, describing Venus' control of 'the heart, the innermost feelings' (Clementi, notes *ad loc.*) ; rather it evokes her grip upon both the body and the emotions, while *mentem* refers to the mind or intellect.
permeanti spiritu. I am not convinced, with Clementi and Schilling, that this is necessarily a translation of the Stoic πνεύματος τινος διὰ παντὸς διήκοντος αὐτοῦ (Arnim, *Vet. Stoic. Frag.* II, 441). Certainly the Stoic *anima mundi* is described as *spiritus* in Latin (cf. Sen., *Nat. Quaest.* II, 45) but so also, in Christian literature, is the Third Person of the Trinity ! For the use of *permeans* to describe divine omnipresence, cf. Apul., *De Mundo*, XXV, 334 : *sed cum credamus deum per omnia permeare.* Apuleius was certainly no Stoic. Cf. too *Corp. Herm : Asclepius* 17 (Nock-Festugière, II, 315) : *Spiritu vero agitantur sive gubernantur omnes in mundo species, unaquaeque secundum naturam suam a deo distributam sibi.* This is indeed far closer to the *Pervigilium* than anything in Stoic philosophy, for God and the spirit are not, like the *anima mundi*, indivisible, but the spirit is the means through which God, a distinct personality, animates the universe.

Valgiglio's defence of *permeante* (TV) betrays ignorance of prosody for, except as an occasional license in Republican verse (also in Virgil), short final vowels are hardly ever followed by a double consonant (other than mute-and-liquid combinations) at the beginning of the next word ; the

Roman ear seems to have found either lengthening, or retention, of the natural quantity equally distasteful in this position.

64. *intus* : the use of this adverb in close association with *spitiru* is compared by Clementi and Schilling with *Aen*. VI, 724-7, where there can be doubt that Virgil is developing a Stoic view of creation :

> *principio caelum et terras camposque liquentes*
> *lucentemque globum lunae Titaniaque astra*
> *spiritus intus alit, totamque infusa per artus*
> *mens agitat molem et magno se corpore miscet.*

That the *Pervigilium* here contains a Virgilian reminiscence is likely, but this scarcely amounts to evidence for Stoic influence, except in the vaguest and most indirect fashion. The syntactical differences, moreover, are significant. *Intus*, in the *Pervigilium*, qualifies a verb with a personal subject, *procreatrix*, whereas Virgil makes *spiritus*, relegated to become an instrumental ablative by our poet, the subject of the predicate *intus alit*. We are not dealing here merely with differences of expression but with a fundamental divergence of thought : between an anthropomorphic, and impersonal, conception of divine activity.
occultis ... viribus. Cf. Apul., *De Mundo* XXX, 358 : *curatque omnibus occulta vis.*
procreatrix : rare but classical, cf. Cic., *De Or*. I, 3, 9 : *philosophia artium procreatrix.*

65. *subditum* : attracted into the singular by *pontum*, but to be taken with *caelum* and *terras* as well : 'through heaven, earth and sea, all subject to her power'.

66. *pervium sui tenorem* : I think this particular phrase may derive from the Stoic concept : ὁ διήκων πνευματικὸς τόνος (cf. Clem. Alex., *Stromata* V, 8, 48, quoted by Clementi), although I would hesitate to assume direct contact with a Greek source. The use of *pervius* in an active sense, as a virtual synonym of *permeans*, is almost unparalleled, but cf. the reference to a *pervius ensis* in Sil., X, 248 (quoted by Schilling). *Tenor* means 'a holding fast', 'an uninterrupted course', and the line is perhaps best paraphrased 'she has fixed (*inbuit* from 67) a permeant and permanent impress of herself in the passage of the seed (*seminali tramite*)' ; i.e. she has imparted her essential power to the movement of seeds, so that they become potent and generate life. Cf. Apul., *De Mundo* XXXVI, 369 : *dum speculatur ad omnia rector eius* (i.e. *mundi*) *atque immutabiliter incumbit*

spargiturque vis illa seminibus inclusa per naturas omnium speciesque et genera digesta. This stanza contains technical language, which is intended, as I hope the notes show, to impart a 'philosophical', rather than an exclusively 'stoical', colour to the passage.

STANZA VIII : VENUS IN HISTORY

Venus is now celebrated as the divine ancestress of the Roman people : *Aeneadum genetrix*. If the poet had belonged to an imperial court, then I would have expected this aspect of her influence to make an earlier, and more emphatic, appearance. Following the poetic grandeur of the previous stanza, these legendary details seem rather flat and the lines quite lack the evocative power of the poem as a whole. And yet they are full of interest, for the descent of the Roman people, with at least two notable stories of rape, is not particularly promising material for a poet praising Venus as the moral inspiration of the universe. Both these episodes are mentioned, but the careless reader would scarcely guess their real nature ; he would think that Venus gave Rhea Silvia, as a young virgin like the nymphs of stanza IV, in marriage to Mars, and he would never suspect the true facts about the union of the Romans and Sabines (cf. notes on lines 71-2). The poet distorts legend, so that he can glorify Venus, as she has been glorified elsewhere in the *Pervigilium*. Although less impressive than other stanzas, we can still observe here the activity of a keen poetic intelligence, carefully moulding the presentation of material to suit the general purpose of the *Pervigilium*.

69. *nepotes*. Rivinus' *penates*, adopted by Riese, is without justification, for this stanza is, above all, concerned with people, the people who, through Venus' aid and inspiration, created the Roman nation. *Nepotes*, apart from its MSS authority, is thus the more appropriate reading : 'Venus transformed her Trojan descendants into Latins'. This first line summarises the process which is dealt with at greater length in the further course of the stanza.

70. *Laurentem puellam* : Lavinia, the daughter of Latinus, given in marriage to Aeneas after he had killed his rival Turnus.

71. The poet is alluding to the rape of Rhea Silvia, the vestal virgin, by Mars, an encounter which bore fruit in the twins Romulus and Remus. The verb *do* frequently means 'to give in marriage' ; the phrase *dat pudicam*

virginem therefore conceals the true nature of the union, particularly as *pudica virgo* here suggests a blushing maiden rather than a consecrated virgin.

72. A reference to the rape of the Sabine women, cf. Ovid's delightful account in *A.A.* I, 101-30, also Livy, I, 9, 1-16. The phrase *fecit nuptias* represents a distortion of the real facts of the incident.

    Romuleas. The long third syllable violates the rule that when two vowels occur together without forming a dipthong the first vowel is always short (for the principal exceptions, cf. D. S. Raven, *Latin Metre*, 24). Clementi is followed by Schilling in comparing this with Hor. *Carm.* II, 20, 13 (*Daidaleo Icaro*) and IV, 2, 2 (*ope Daidalea*), but these are unsatisfactory analogies as Greek derivatives frequently have long vowels in this position, a consideration which justifies Horace's decision to regard the third syllable as metrically long. A Grilli (*PP* 24 (1969), 50) compares the scansion of Iuleus (cf. Ov., *Fast.* IV, 124 ; V, 564 ; VI, 797) with a long ē, but, although this is more promising than *Daidaleus*, I personally doubt whether the poet is preceding by analogy ; it seems more likely that this metrical irregularity is either a slip or a deliberate licence taken without conscious appeal to any precedent.

    Ramnes et Quirites. Schilling convincingly explains why the poet only mentions two of the three ancient Roman tribes mentioned by Livy (I, 13, 8) ; because the third tribe the *Luceres*, 'échappent au lien matrimonial sanctionné par Vénus', and secondly because, 'la tradition romaine a toujours plus insisté sur la fusion des Romains et des Sabines'. Cf. further, Schilling *ad loc*. *Ramnes* refers to the ancient Latin stock, while *Quirites* represent the Sabine element in the early Roman state. The presence of the *Luceres*, here unmentioned, acknowledges an admixture of Etruscan blood in the veins of the early Romans.

74. † *Romuli matrem* † *crearet et nepotem Caesarem.* This line is, in my opinion, an insoluble *crux*, although numerous attempts have been made either to justify the reading of the MSS, or to solve its problems by emendation. As the MSS stand *Romuli matrem* should naturally be taken as an allusion to Rhea Silvia, but she has already been mentioned in 71 and this further reference introduces an intolerable confusion into the chronological sequence of the stanza, as does Baehrens' transposition of 73-4 to follow 70.

    The majority of editors from Lipsius onwards have seen in line 74 a tribute to the *gens Julia* as the consummation of Venus' activity on behalf

of the Roman people. This necessarily involves emendation, as Crusius'
contention that *matrem* refers to Julia, the sister of Julius and grand-
mother of Augustus, is absurd ; it is surely unthinkable that our poet
would in this fashion arbitrarily fasten upon a rather obscure member of
the gens *Iulia*.

Scholars who defend the MSS reading seek the chronological key of the
Pervigilium in this line of the poem. Rand (*REL*, 91-3) argues that Trajan
might appropriately have been considered a *Romulus redivivus*, and thus
identifies *matrem* with the mother of Trajan, while referring *nepotem
Caesarem* to Antoninus Pius, the adopted son of Hadrian. The poem is
placed in the reign of Antoninus (138-61). D. S. Robertson (*CR* (1938),
109-12) suggested that the line is a compliment to Romula, mother of the
emperor Galerius (who − cf. Lactantius, *De Mort. Pers.* IX, 8 − claimed to
be an *alter Romulus*) and Maximinus Daia, her grandson, officially
designated *Caesar* during the years 305-9. This places the *Pervigilium* in
the early years of the fourth century, and Robertson suggests a specific
occasion for its composition : the betrothal of Candidianus, the son of
Galerius, to the daughter of Maximinus in 307. An anonymous scholar
writing under the initials 'G.F.' (*Jahr. class. Phil.* CV (1872), 494) dated
the poem to 476 A.D. on the theory that line 75 mentions Julius Nepos
(*Nepotem Caesarem*) and the mother of Romulus Augustulus.

Rand's date is too early (cf. 'Date and Authorship', p. 19) and the
reference to Trajan's mother, an obscure Spaniard, is out of place,
especially in the reign of Antoninus. The thesis of Robertson is a
monument to misplaced ingenuity. Only a poet associated with the
immediate imperial circle would have been interested in, or perhaps even
aware of, the family ties binding Romula, Galerius and Maximinus.
Assuming then that the *Pervigilium* was written by a court poet for a
court occasion, why does the poet exalt Romula and Maximinus at the
expense of Galerius, why is there only this long-delayed and insultingly
short tribute to the poet's patrons, and why is there no direct reference
(unless lost in the MSS transmission) to the event which the *Pervigilium*
supposedly celebrates ? The argument of 'G.F.' is even less convincing,
for Romulus Augustulus was the son of Orestes of Pannonia, the very
man who drove Nepos from Rome in 476. What circumstances would
lead a court poet so dangerously to confuse hostile parties, and who but a
court poet would consider presenting either Romulus or Nepos as
evidence of Venus' continuing favour to the people of Rome ?

That a poet should associate the imperial family of his day with the activity of a goddess whose influence has been traced back to the earliest era of Roman legend, is not as absurd as Schilling seems to suggest (XXII-V), but the attempts of scholars to interpret the MSS reading here as a reference to the dynasty in power at the time of the poem's composition are all unsatisfactory (I have dealt only with the more plausible theories ; for further speculation of this type, cf. Clementi 78-82) ; moreover the *Pervigilium* nowhere else betrays any affinity with the work of imperial propagandists. Roman panegyric, even when not absurd, is neither obscure nor allusive, and I am convinced that even a passing compliment by a poet without a position at court would have been more boldly advertised than here in the *Pervigilium*.

I am, therefore, in litle doubt that *nepotem Caesarem* describes Augustus, the first Roman emperor, especially since the *gens Iulia* traced their ancestry back to Aeneas (cf. line 70), the son of Venus herself. The poet is celebrating the power of Venus as revealed in the pageant of Roman legend and history, particularly in the descent of the line she founded, which culminates in the emergence of Augustus as creator of the imperial system.

But *matrem* cannot stand. The line originally probably mentioned Julius as well as Augustus Caesar ; Wernsdorf, Clementi and Schilling are all of this opinion and adopt Lipsius' conjecture *patrem* :

> *proque prole posterum*
> *Romuli, patrem crearet et nepotem Caesarem.*

But two important objections incline me against acceptance of this emendation. Firstly that it necessitates punctuation before *patrem* and thus creates the long and clumsy phrase *proque prole posterum Romuli*. I hesitate to introduce this into the text of a poem of such delicate, and generally economical, expression as the *Pervigilium*. Moreover enjambement does not occur elsewhere in the *Pervigilium* ; this is used by Clementi and Schilling to explain the corruption, cf. Schilling *ad loc* : 'le copiste, habitué à voir le sens de la phrase finir avec le vers, a méconnu le rejet *Romuli* ; il a relié *Romuli patrem* (i.e. *Martem*, obviously out of place in this context) et s'est empressé de corriger cette 'faute' en écrivant '*Romuli matrem*''. This argument would be more convincing if the admission of an unprecedented enjambement produced an apt or elegant phrase, instead of one which is ugly and superfluous.

How are we, secondly, meant to interpret the juxtaposition of *patrem* and *nepotem* ? Schilling believes that *patrem* describes Julius as the father of the first imperial line through adoption of Augustus, while *nepotem* represents Augustus' right, as nephew of Julius, to be considered a descendant of Venus. But I think it more likely that a poet would describe *either* the real *or* the adoptive relationship, rather than a compressed admixture of both. *Pater* naturally expects to be complemented by *filius*, not by *nepos*, and it was precisely as *divi filius* that Augustus justified his rise to power (cf. *R.G.* I, 2). Schilling supports *patrem* by comparison with Ov., *Fast.* III, 709-10 :

> hoc opus, haec pietas, haec prima elementa fuerunt
>   Caesaris, ulcisci iusta per arma patrem.

But this assumes the very relationship which *nepotem* so jarringly denies. I find it difficult to believe that a poet wishing to mention both Julius and Augustus Caesar as members of the *gens Iulia* and descendants of Venus, would choose, while describing Julius as *pater*, then to emphasise the real blood-relationship rather than the adoptive one of father and son.

Bury (*CR* XIX (1905), 304) places a comma, like Lipsius, after *Romuli* and reads *mater* for *matrem*, but this involves enjambement with all its attendant difficulties and throws a not impossible, but unpleasant, force upon the necessarily emphatic *et* ; nor do I feel Venus' status as *mater* is in particular need of assertion here. Fort's *Romuli parem* is more likely, but the honour of this tribute would more appropriately have been conferred on Augustus than Julius. Other attempts to restore the text are entirely fanciful and involve drastic alteration : *Iliae gentem* (Brakman), *unde, prolem posterum, Romuli gentem* (Riese).

In this line reference is probably made to Julius and Augustus Caesar, but the labours of scholarship have not produced a convincing restoration. I have, therefore, obelised *Romuli matrem*, although corruption may extend further.

Stanza IX : Venus in Nature

Venus is here celebrated as a goddess of rural fertility, a *rôle* which reflects her original nature before its assimilation into the person of Aphrodite. *Amor* too is reintroduced, but without any hint of the threat which his presence signified in earlier stanzas. The poet perhaps wishes to suggest another aspect of Venus' motherhood ; seen in stanza VII as the cosmic *procreatrix*, in VIII as *Aeneadum genetrix* and the patroness of the

Roman people, she now appears almost as an ordinary mother with her child : she herself shares the emotions she inspires.

The function of the stanza is also transitional ; the rural setting and the personification of natural processes take us back to the poem's starting point in lines 1-4, and prepare the way for the fundamental contrast of the final stanza : between the loud joy of nature in love and the silent grief of the lonely poet.

76. *voluptas*. Cf. Lucretius, I, 1 :

> *Aeneadum genetrix, hominum divumque voluptas.*

Also Ov., *Fast*. IV, 99.

77. *Amor ... rure natus dicitur*. Cf. Tib., II, 1, 67-8 :

> *ipse quoque inter agros interque armenta Cupido*
> *natus, et indomitas dicitur inter equas.*

78. *ager cum parturiret* : Clementi is right to insist that this phrase does not mean that the fields themselves gave birth to Cupid, but is a periphrasis for *verno tempore*. The personification is fairly commonplace, cf. Virg., *Georg*., II, 330 ; Pentadius, *A.L.* 235, 3.

79. *florum delicatis educavit osculis*. Clementi translates, 'foster'd him with dainty kisses that on roses' lips he pressed'. But this does violence to the Latin which must mean : 'She nourished him on the tender kisses of the flowers'. How are we to interpret this ? The poet is probably being deliberately impressionistic, reversing the statement in 23 that the roses were made from the kisses of Amor. Perhaps *delicatis osculis* is a poetic way of expressing Amor's nourishment from the drops of dew which gather on flowers. The primary force of *educo* here must be of physical support, but perhaps the notion of mental training is also implicit : even Amor's earliest days were spent in a world of miniature passion where he began to encounter and understand the emotions he was later to exploit so skilfully.

Stanza X : Fulfilment and Isolation

In stanza I the poet declared : *vere concordant amores*. This statement is now realised in a picture of pastoral bliss which conveys a feeling of complete, almost careless, emotional security. Line 2 insisted *ver iam canorum* ; the landscape is now suddenly filled with song, with the raucous chatter of swans and the melodious music of the nightingale and the swallow. It is the singing of Philomela, and Procne (suffering women as well as singing birds) which provokes the poet's self-examination and produces the poem's unexpected conclusion in grief and silence.

These two birds enjoy a long and fascinating history in classical literature (cf. Raby (1951) who traces their career from Homer down into the Middle Ages); throughout its course their song communicates a poignant message of suffering and sin, while it is a traditional feature of any spring scene and is more rarely, with no hint of its traditional burden, heard by poets as a carol of pure joy (cf. Meleager, *A.P.* IX, 363). These different threads are gathered together, and woven into the tapestry of the *Pervigilium*, with marvellous effect.

Of fundamental importance is the poet's insistence upon the mythological significance of both the swallow and the nightingale, for this concentrates our attention upon two suffering individuals and their tragic history. So far the *Pervigilium* has celebrated love as a force of universal creativity. But the marriage of Tereus and Philomela, with the husband's brutal infidelity and the wife's savage vengeance, represents the perversion of the very principle which the *Pervigilium* exalts. It is in this context that the poet suggests a transformation far more profound than the physical metamorphosis which is the *dénouement* of the legend; he suggests that Philomela has finally found release and sings now not of sorrow and loss but in joyful celebration of the *motus amoris*. We seem on the brink of a final affirmation of Venus' power to quicken and transform.

An equally important motif is the idea of silence become song; the poet encounters this in the person of Procne, the sister, who has escaped from the long silence which was Tereus' brutal gift to her, and, as the swallow, can join in Nature's spring song. Again the poet implies or imagines that emotional transformation has accompanied physical change.

In the song of the nightingale and the swallow, and in the story associated with them, the poet confronts a world of destructive emotion and endless sorrow. At the same time he grasps at the possibility of change, of hatred becoming love, of silence becoming song. It is this which inspires his longing for a personal spring, a prayer which expresses his yearning for experience of the transforming power which he imagines to have released Philomela and Procne from their human misery. The manner in which physical metamorphosis embodies the possibility, and the poet's own need, of an emotional revolution, the way, moreover, in which legend casts dark shadows over the radiant landscape of the

Pervigilium, represents the most complex and evocative reaction in classical literature to the song of Procne and Philomela. And yet the allusion does not, as Wilhelm (1965, p. 28) suggests, inspire the poet's rejection of his vision, but intensifies its impact ; what was an expression of uncomplicated faith in a metaphysical reality, is suddenly felt, both by the poet and his reader, as an urgent emotional necessity ; the final refrain is no longer anticipation or command, but a poignant call for help – *de profundis*.

The poet's silence echoes through the closing lines of the poem. His insistence upon it is puzzling, especially when, as Wilhelm observes (p. 28), he has just written 90 of the most memorable lines in Latin literature. Cazzaniga (1955) suggests a simple interpretation : the poet has finished his song and is faced with the prospect of silence. But what of the question : *quando ver venit meum* ? This speaks to me of the longing for something never experienced before.

> *quando fiam uti chelidon ut tacere desinam ?*

This is not the prayer of one contemplating silence in the future, but an appeal for release from a long and unwilling silence.

> *perdidi Musam tacendo nec me Phoebus respicit.*

This is the statement of a penitent who blames himself and his past, not his gods, for what has happened to him. The poet clearly does not regard silence as an imminent prospect, but as a continuing spiritual condition from which he prays deliverance.

Spring and song have been associated since line 2. Song is creation's affirmation of the power of love, nor can the poet imagine that the nightingale or swallow sings of anything but love. But himself he feels no spring and can only contemplate, in the world about him, those qualities of soul for which he longs. His yearning for spring and his prayer for the power of song are one and the same, for his silence will be ended when he feels the quickening touch of love and can join the whole of nature in its celebration of the omnipotence of the goddess.

81. *subter*. The MSS read *super* but Broukhusius (1708) confirmed his emendation by reference to Calp. Sic., I, 1, 4-5 :

> *cernis ut, ecce, pater quas tradidit, Ornyte, vaccae*
> *molle sub hirsuta latus explicuere genesta.*

Mackail preserves *super* and Valgiglio believes that *subter* is not absolutely necessary arguing that the shade of *umiles genestae* (cf. Virg.,

Georg. II, 435), while it might offer shelter to sheep or shepherds, could scarcely provide a comfortable retreat for the *tauri* which Scaliger's emendation introduces into the line (for which cf. below). But if the sheep, in line 83, seek sanctuary in the shade from the heat of the sun, these are foolhardy bulls who expose themselves so rashly on top of the brooms. Moreover the bulls, as the following line reveals, are lying with their mates ; lovers, in literature and, I imagine, in real-life, seek a measure of privacy for their dalliance, and would prefer the shade, even of a humble broom-tree, to the all-revealing glare of the sun.

tauri : Scaliger's emendation for *aonii* in the MSS ; the process of corruption is convincingly explained by Valgiglio as stemming from omission of the initial 't' through haplography. Lipsius' *agni* makes nonsense of the marital *foedus* in 82, while Baehren's *apri* is also inappropriate in a context which requires mention of pastoral animals which graze, or rest, in herds.

82. *tutus quo tenetur coniugali foedere* : this is the reading of S (with *federe* for *foedere*). The proposed emendations of Baehrens (*torvus* for *tutus*) and Lipsius (*quisque coetus continetur*, accepted by Rivinus and Mackail) are inferior as well as unnecessary, for *tutus* emphasises the emotional security which the poet imagines to be a quality of the love Venus inspires.

85. This line, as previous editors have realised, derives from Virg., *Aen*. XI, 458 :

> *dant sonitum rauci per stagna loquacia cycni.*

If use of the epithet *raucus* does not (cf. Schilling *ad loc*.) exclude the swans from the ranks of melodious birds, its employment together with *loquaces* suggests the clamorous shouts of affirmation with which they greet the summons of the goddess communicated in 84.

Wilhelm is mistaken to identify their singing here with the dying song of the prophetic swan (for which cf. Cic., *Tusc*. I, 30, 73). Although swan-song is often associated with imminent death, the swan is also a bird of Venus ; a team of swans draw her chariot to the house of the bride Violentilla (Statius, *Silv*. I, 2, 140-2) and, in this context, their singing conveys no hint of melancholy :

> *pandit nitidos domus alta penates*
> *claraque gaudentes plauserunt limina cycni.*   (145-6)

It is to this tradition which the swan-song of the *Pervigilium* belongs.

86-90. These lines mention two birds ; *chelidon* is a graecism for *hirundo*, the
swallow, while *Terei puella* must be an allusion to the nightingale, not, as
Wilhelm claims, to the swallow, for the nightingale is a bird which sings
in the shade (cf. Cat., 65, 13-14) and line 86, with its specific reference to
poplar shade, clearly recalls Virgil's famous description of Philomel's song
in *Georg.* IV, 511-15. The swallow, on the other hand, makes its home
among rooftops, cf. Vespa, *A.L.* 199, 54-5 (the miller is condemning the
craft of the cook) :

> *tu facis in lucis ut cantet tristis aëdon*
> *maestaque sub tecto sua murmuret acta chelidon.*

Lines 86-8 have traditionally been interpreted as a description of the
song of the nightingale alone (cf. below for the versions of Schilling and
Rand). On this assumption *illa cantat* must refer to the nightingale. But
why then does the poet suddenly forget Philomela and ask 'when will I be
like the swallow ?' The two birds, it is true, are mythological sisters and
the poet's meditation upon the significance of Philomel's song might be
imagined to have provoked the allusion to her sister. But the fact that the
poet suddenly deserts his emphatic insistence upon the song of the
nightingale and longs instead for the voice of a swallow still amounts to a
strange and unsatisfying transition.

And yet the fault lies with editors of the *Pervigilium* and not with the
poet himself, for line 88, I think, introduces the song of the swallow, and
illa cantat is a reference, not to the nightingale, but to Procne, her sister.
Mention of *chelidon* in 90 is far more powerful if we have already met the
swallow, while the singular *illa cantat* (of the swallow alone) is explained
by an important aspect of Procne's mythological experience not shared by
Philomela (cf. notes to 89).

Scholars who believe that only one bird sings in 86-88 offer no
satisfactory interpretation of 88 ; Schilling takes *sororem* as the object of
queri and renders the line : 'on ne dirait pas qu'elle (i.e. rossignol) plaint
une sœur, victime de son barbare époux'. This is not syntactically
impossible, but it forces the Latin into a very awkward mould. Moreover
throughout classical literature the song of the nightingale communicates a
message of *personal* grief as the anguished voice of a suffering and sinful
mother ; I do not think it likely that our poet, to whom song is a revelation
of the inner self, would here unaccountably represent the traditional
burden of Philomel's song as an expression of sympathy with the
suffering of another, even of her sister.

Rand (*TAPhA* (1934), 1-12) interprets *sororem*, not as the object, but as the subject of *queri* in the accusative and infinitive construction and as a further reference to *Terei puella*. He paraphrases : 'Her song, for once, is not of her ancient grief against her barbarian spouse'. But why then is *sororem* here at all and why again has the poet deserted the lyric tradition which hears, in the nightingale's song, a mother's lament for the self-inflicted loss of her son ?

The nightingale sings in 86, the swallow in 90. Should we not, therefore, take *sororem* as the subject of *queri* referring, not to the nightingale, but to the sister of *Terei puella*, Procne, the swallow ? This is at once the easiest and most natural interpretation of the Latin, and the one best suited to the highly evocative context in which line 88 occurs. For a similar introduction of the swallow as *soror*, cf. *Aetna*, 587-9 :

> *Philomela canoris*
> *evocat in silvis et tu, soror, hospita tectis*
> *acciperis, solis Tereus ferus exsulat agris.*

We can now paraphrase 86-8 as follows : 'Tereus' wife, Philomela the nightingale, is singing in the shade ; you would think that she sang the motions of love (and did not mourn for her dead son) ; you would deny that her sister, Procne the swallow, was lamenting a brutal lover'. Alone among editors Cazzaniga recognises two voices in 86-8 ; since this is a mere assumption on his part, I have thought these lines deserved detailed discussion.

86. *Terei puella* : this must be the wife of Tereus and not her sister, as Clementi believes, for when the poet, in line 90, longs like the swallow, to end his silence, he is obviously referring to an important detail of the Philomela-Procne myth, in which Tereus, having raped his wife's sister, tore out her tongue to ensure her silence ; it was only through metamorphosis that she found her voice again. The poet longs for a similar, but spiritual, transformation. Since, therefore, the swallow is the violated sister, *Terei puella*, the nightingale, must be the wife, not the unwilling mistress, of Tereus.

88. *marito barbaro*. For *maritus* of a lover or suitor, not a husband, cf. *Aen.* IV, 35 :

> (Didonem) *aegram nulli quondom flexere mariti.*

Tereus was, of course, in no sense an ordinary lover : this is the point of *barbaro*. The phrase provides a significant contrast with the moral power of love on which the poet has previously dwelt.

89. *illa cantat, nos tacemus*. Cazzaniga writes : 'Canta di gioia la rondine (e canta anche l'usignolo ; 89 'illa cantat' vale per l'uno e l'altro), immemore del dolore'. This is incorrect and ignores that important incident discussed in the notes to 86 : the silence which was brutally imposed upon Procne and from which she escaped through transformation. The poet is concentrating upon a particular, and, to him, very significant aspect of the myth. In the song of the nightingale and the swallow, in the tragic history which it calls to mind, he not only imagines grief become joy, but encounters, in the swallow, an equally fundamental metamorphosis : silence become song ; hence the singular *illa cantat* which refers to the swallow alone.

venit. Jachmann's suggested emendation, *veniet* (cf. Cazzaniga, 80, n. 3), is totally unnecessary, cf. Mart., V, 58, 1-2 :

> *cras te victurum, cras dicis, Postume, semper.*
> *dic mihi, cras istud, Postume, quando venit.*

90. *fiam* : the reading of S, preferable to *faciam* because :

   a) *Faciam uti* introduces a tribrach into the 2nd foot, a usage which does not occur elsewhere, although we find a solitary tribrach in the 3rd foot of line 31.

   b) The poet is thinking of transformation through experience of the power of love. This will awake a spring of the soul and will transform the poet, as Procne was transformed. The passive form, stressing inner change and experience, is therefore more appropriate.

uti : Rivinus' emendation *metri causa* for *ut* in the MSS. Hiatus is not admissible in this position.

ut : after *uti* the *ut* of a result clause may not be particularly elegant, but this scarcely seems a sufficient justification for Cazzaniga's *et*.

91. *Phoebus*. Rivinus, followed by Clementi, avoids the fifth-foot spondee by substituting *Apollo* for *Phoebus* ; there is, of course, no justification for this emendation, cf. metrical discussion, pp. 36-40.

92. The silence of *Amyclae* and its subsequent destruction are proverbial in Latin literature (for references cf. Clementi, *ad loc.*) and Servius (ad *Aen.* X, 564) offers five alternative explanations for the origin of the association. We meet two towns in antiquity called *Amyclae*, in Laconia ('Αμύχλαι) and in Latium. The fact that the silence-story is a Roman tradition and that the epithet *tacitae* is only applied by very late authors (cf. Aus., *Ep*. XXIX, 26 ; Dracontius, *Rom*. VIII, 435-9) to the Greek township, suggests that the tradition of destruction through silence belongs to the Italian *Amyclae*.

The Achievement of the *Pervigilium*

R. R. Bolgar ([1]) has written of the *Pervigilium* that, 'the longing for a magical rebirth, that external salvation which has always been the comfort of the helpless, finds expression through the etiolated prettiness of the familiar worship of Love. The emotion which sprang from a deep contemporary need and the shop-worn trappings which poets had used for centuries with no background of feeling sit uneasily together. The result is a work which leaves the reader with a slight discomfort, as if he were suspended between two worlds'. I consider this view, that the *Pervigilium* is an unsatisfactory expression of a profound emotional need, that art fails in the service of life, to be mistaken. Most Latin poetry, from the silver age onwards until the rise of a Christian literature, can fairly be said to have been stifled by a tradition which had long been stale. But the *Pervigilium* is an exception ; for here the effect of a rich heritage stimulating a serious purpose is dynamic and exciting. I hope that the truth of this claim is supported by my discussion of individual stanzas, where I have tried to show that the poet is always the master, and never the slave, of tradition, that he enriches and revivifies the traditions upon which he draws, that ideas are stated, juxtaposed and developed to form a powerful and coherent poetic complex. Particularly exhilarating is the sheer range of the poet's vision which embraces the visual charm and profound symbolism of stanza III, the solemn and vibrant joy anticipated in the festival stanzas, the mythological grandeur of stanzas II and VII,

---

(1) R. R. BOLGAR, *The Classical Heritage* (Cambridge, 1954) 23 ; this is only a passing reference to the *P.V.*, in a work which is not concerned with literary criticism. I quote this passage, not in a contentious spirit, but because it provides a useful springboard for my final assessment of the *Pervigilium*. For a detailed, and highly unsatisfactory, interpretation of the poem as literature, cf. J. J. WILHELM, *The Cruelest Month* (Yale, 1965), 20f. Wilhelm uses Clementi's 1936 text, in which the sequence of the poem is disrupted by violent transposition ; his treatment of the *P.V.*, moreover, is a compound of carelessness, misinterpretation of the Latin, frequent self-contradiction and pervasive superficiality dressed up in critical jargon. One or two remarks betray some insight.

and the emotional immediacy of lines 81-88. The festival itself is thus set in a deep perspective of ideas and emotions, which expresses the yearnings of the individual in terms of universal and living truth.

And yet we cannot read the *Pervigilium* without a sense of discomfort, but this discomfort springs from a far deeper conflict than any struggle between emotional need and its artistic communication. The tension is a religious one : between faith and experience. For the *Pervigilium* is a statement of faith and, as such, is far more than a song of praise : it is an expression of, and a response to, a profound spiritual want, namely the need of the individual to assimilate himself to a reality larger and more satisfying than the self. The poet attempts this through identification with nature's self-renewal, a process which is interpreted as the effulgence of the divine splendour, but the chant of the nightingale tolls the poet back to his sole self, and he is denied escape into any experience broader than his own.

But the poet's personal failure does not lead, as Wilhelm has suggested, to his rejection of the vision which precedes it ; for the truth of this vision, the possibility of salvation, is far more important to a lonely and suffering individual than it would have been to someone who could share with uncomplicated joy in nature's universal experience. Such a person would never have written the *Pervigilium* which is both a vision of hope and an urgent cry for help : 'quamdiu, quamdiu ? "cras et cras ?" quare non modo ?'

Thus the discomfort which the poem calls forth is not the result of literary inadequacy but derives from a reverberating tension between a metaphysical interpretation of nature and the discordant presence of an individual who cannot embrace his creation of faith ; this conflict is the poem's *raison d'être*, and the power with which it is communicated represents the poet's artistic achievement.

The reason for the failure of the poet to find salvation in the religion of Venus is that, rooted in sexual feeling, his vision is of an immanent rather than a truly transcendent force. His search does not take him *beyond* nature ; nature itself is Venus' gospel and revelation, which makes it almost inevitable that he should turn to consider his own place within nature. Contrast this with the magnificent Easter hymn of Venantius Fortunatus (*Salve festa dies*, Leo III, 9), and the difference between worship of the immanent and the transcendent will perhaps emerge more clearly ; for Fortunatus begins with nature, with the vigour and tumult of spring, but landscape expresses the cosmic response to an event which eclipsed the cycle and violated the laws of nature, an event which sweeps the believer far beyond natural processes to the contemplation of a spiritual and eternal reality, against which his personal experience in creation can have little significance beyond the response of faith. It is not surprising then to find that Fortunatus merges inobtrusively into his landscape, chirping away as a humble sparrow for love of his lord :

> *si tibi nunc avium resonant virgulta susurro,*
> *has inter minimus passer amore cano.*   (45-6)

Again the *Pervigilium* begins with the universal, the poet is apparently preoccupied with the universal and only stumbles accidentally upon personal experience, but the movement is nevertheless towards the self. In contrast the progress of Boethius, in his spiritual autobiography, the *Consolatio Philosophiae*, leads away from the individual. Beginning in self-absorption, in misery and defeat, the *Consolatio* follows the rise of the human spirit from introverted dejection to find salvation through knowledge and contemplation of the divine love which governs and inspires the universe. Thus II, VIII, a hymn to the spirit of love, celebrates *caelo imperitans amor* (15) as the force which preserves order in diversity, which breathes love and concord into the life of man :

> *hic sancto populos quoque*
> *iunctos foedere continet,*
> *hic et coniugii sacrum*
> *castis nectit amoribus,*
> *hic fidis etiam sua*
> *dictat iura sodalibus.*
> *o felix hominum genus,*
> *si vestros animos amor*
> *quo caelum regitur, regat.*   (22-30)

Our existence upon earth can be touched by, and can itself express the divine love which moderates creation. It is the perception of this ruling spirit which rescues Boethius from the despair of his first poem, and leads him to perceive, beyond the confusion, suffering and injustice which beset the individual upon earth, a force of order, of stability and love, which binds together the universe with ties of mutual affection (IV, VI, 44-8). Salvation, for Boethius, is the process by which the mind frees itself from the *tenebrae* and *terreni flatus* of our existence upon earth and, rising to enjoy once more its *propria lux*, paces in contemplation among the stars.

Here, once again, we realise why the poet of the *Pervigilium* fails to embrace his vision of love, for not only is it earth-bound, but is dangerously close to a mere projection of personal yearning and emotion ; the poet cannot rise above himself in a quest of the spirit and the intellect which takes the individual beyond self in the contemplation of divinity. Instead he impresses the marks of his own personality upon nature, he imagines that nature enjoys the fulfilment he longs for ; his interpretation of spring thus inevitably leads to its personal application and the poet cannot finally rise to heaven and lose himself in worship, but confronts the darkness which lies at the heart of his vision, the darkness of the lonely, silent and suffering self.

It might be objected that the Christian hymn and Boethian platonism is company too elevated for the *Pervigilium Veneris*. Mackail, at any rate, who declared that in the *Pervigilium* 'poetry had gone back to childhood', would almost certainly have denied that the *Pervigilium* belonged to the poetry of serious ideas. In my discussion of the poem I have frequently insisted upon its conceptual gravity, without, I hope, implying that grace and charm do not represent a significant measure of its appeal. And yet the greatness of the *Pervigilium* does not, of course, reside in its philosophy, but in the power with which it expresses both a vision of hope and the dilemma which attends the frustration of this hope. It is here that the world of Fortunatus and Boethius is the world of the *Pervigilium*, a world where the individual desperately feels the need of salvation from beyond the self. The poem communicates a spiritual crisis far deeper than that of thwarted sexuality, for the poet's intensely felt but unfulfilled desire to share the life of nature emphasises his profound sense of alienation from, and his pressing need to feel at one with, the world he inhabits. His failure to find salvation is, as we have seen, due to more than personal circumstances, for it is the flawed and limited nature of his vision which makes these circumstances important. But it is the poet's very failure to realise his dream which makes the *Pervigilium Veneris*, as a poem, such an evocative and haunting creation.

BIBLIOGRAPHY

ARNIM J. VON, *Stoicorum Veterum Fragmenta*, IV vols. (Leipzig, 1905-24).

BAEHRENS E., *Poetae Latini Minores*, V vols. (Leipzig, 1879-83) ; *Unedirte lateinische Gedichte* (Leipzig, 1877).

BERGK T., *Commentatio de Pervigilio Veneris* (Halle, 1859).

BOLGAR R. R., *The Classical Heritage* (Cambridge, 1954).

BOUHIER J., 'Lettres ... au R. P. Oudin contenant des remarques sur le *Pervigilium Veneris*', in *Nouvelles Littéraires*, vol. XI (Amsterdam, 1720) ; 1st letter 366-80 ; 2nd 380-92.

BOYANCÉ P., 'Encore sur le *Pervigilium Veneris*', *REL* XXVIII (1950), 212-35.

——, 'Le *Pervigilium Veneris* et les *Veneralia*', *Mélanges A. Piganiol* (Paris, 1966), III, 1547-63.

BRAKMAN C., 'Quando *Pervigilium Veneris* conditum est ?', *Mnemosyne* LVI (1928), 254-70.

BROUKHUSIUS J. *Albii Tibulli equitis Romani quae exstant* (Amsterdam, 1708). For *P.V.* cf. 221.

BUECHELER F., *Pervigilium Veneris* (Leipzig, 1859).

BURY J. B., 'On the *Pervigilium Veneris*', *CR* XIX (1905), 304.

CAZZANIGA I., '*Agni* o *tauri* in *Pervigilium Veneris* V. 81', *RIL* LXXXVII (1954), 271-82.

——, 'Saggio critico ed esegetico sul *Pervigilium Veneris*', *SCO* III (1955), 46-101.

——, 'Il verso 23 del *Pervigilium Veneris* e alcune pitture vascolari', *PP* XLII (1955), 188-95.

——, 'Il *Pervigilium Veneris*', *Nuova Antologia*, November 1956, 331-42.

——, *Carmina Ludicra Romanorum : Pervigilium Veneris, Priapea* (Turin, 1959). Text as in 'Saggio critico' (1955).

CLEMENTI Sir C., *The Pervigilium Veneris*[3] (Oxford, 1936).

CRUSIUS C., *Probabilia Critica* (Leipzig, 1753). For conjectures on the *P.V.* cf. 261-3.

DOUSA MAIOR J., Cf. under Lipsius below.

DOUSA FILIUS J., *Catullus, Tibullus, Propertius : accessit Pervigilium Veneris* (Leyden, 1592).

FORT J. A., *The Pervigilium Veneris in quatrains* (Oxford, 1922).

GRILLI A., '*Pervigilium Veneris* v. 72', *PP* XXIV (1969), 50.

GRISET E., 'Il *Pervigilium Veneris*', *RSC* V (1957), 169-74.

'G.F.', 'Zum *Pervigilium Veneris*', *Jahr. class. Phil.* CV (1872), 494.

HEAD B. V., *Historia Numorum* (Oxford, 1911).

HEINSIUS N., *P. Ovidii Nasonis Operum tomus tertius* (Amsterdam, 1661), cf. 412 for note on line 46 of *P.V.*

——, *Cl. Claudiani quae exstant* (Amsterdam, 1665), cf. 912 for note on line 64 of *P.V.*

HERRMANN L., 'Claudius Antonius et le *Pervigilium Veneris*', *Latomus* XII (1953), 53-69.

LATKOCZY M. VON, *Verfasser und Veranlassung des Pervigilium Veneris* : an unpublished lecture summarised in *Verhandlungen der 42sten Sammlung deutscher Philologen und Schulmänner in Wien vom 24 bis 27 mai 1893* (Teubner, 1894), 225-6.

LAURENTI E., 'De Iulio Annaeo Floro poeta atque historico, *Pervigilii Veneris* auctore', *RFIC* XX (1892), 125-143.

LEUTSCH E. L. VON, SCHEIDEWIN F. G., *Corpus paroemiographorum Graecorum* II vols. (Göttingen, 1839-51).

LIPSIUS J., *Justi Lipsii Electorum Liber* I (Antwerp, 1580) ; cf. 35-46 for Lipsius' treatment of the *P.V.*, where he cites the conjectures of Dousa maior.

MACKAIL J. W., 'The *Pervigilium Veneris*', *Journal of Philology* XVII (1888), 179-91.

——, *Catullus, Tibullus and the Pervigilium Veneris* (London, 1912).

MARTIN G., 'Transposition of verses in the *Pervigilium Veneris*', *CPh* XXX (1935), 255-9.

MUELLER O., *De P. Annio Floro poeta et carmine quod Pervigilium Veneris inscriptum est* (Berlin, 1855).

OWEN S. G., *Catullus, with the Pervigilium Veneris* (London, 1893).

PITHOU P., *Pervigilii Veneris editio princeps* (Paris, 1577).

RABY F. J. E., '*Philomela, praevia temporis amoeni*', *Mélanges J. de Ghellinck* II vols. (Gembloux, 1951), 435-448.

RAND E. K., 'Sur le *Pervigilium Veneris*', *REL* XII (1934), 83-95.

——, 'Spirit and Plan of the *Pervigilium Veneris*', *TAPhA* LXV (1934), 1-12.

RIBBECK O., 'Zum *Pervigilium Veneris*', *RhM* XIV (1859), 324-5.

RICHMOND J. A., *Halieutica* (London, 1962).

RIESE A., *Anthologia Latina sive Poesis Latinae supplementum*, vol. I (Leipzig, 1894).

RIGLER F. A., *Examina Gymnasii Cliviensis ...* (Clèves, 1829).

RIVINUS A., *Elegans et floridum carmen de vere, communiter Pervigilium Veneris inscriptum* (Leipzig and Frankfurt, 1644).

ROBERTSON D. S. 'The Date and Occasion of the *Pervigilium Veneris*', *CR* LII (1938), 109-12.

ROLLO W., 'The date and authorship of the *Pervigilium Veneris*', *CPh* XXIV (1929), 405-8.

ROMANO D., *Pervigilium Veneris* (Palermo, 1952).

SAUMAISE C. de, *Animadversiones in Pervigilium Veneris*, cf. under Scriverius.

SCALIGER J., For Scaliger's notes in one of the two surviving copies of the *editio princeps*, cf. H. OMONT, 'Conjectures de Joseph Scaliger sur le *Pervigilium Veneris*', *RPh* IX (1885), 124-6.

SCHENKL H., 'Zur Kritik und Überlieferungsgeschichte des Grattius und anderer lateinischer Dichter', *JKPh* suppl. XXIV (1898), 387-480.

SCHENKL K., 'Zur Kritik des *Pervigilium Veneris*', *Zeit. für die österreichischen Gymnasien* XVIII (1867), 233-43.

——, *ibid*. XX (1871), 127-8. Collation of Vind. 9401 against Buecheler's text.

——, 'Zu lateinischen Anthologie', *WS* I (1879), 59-62.

SCHILLING R., *La Veillée de Vénus* (Paris, 1944).

——, 'En reprenant le *Pervigilium Veneris*', *Kokalos* XIII (1967), 3-18.

SCRIVERIUS P., *Pervigilii Veneris nova editio auctior et emendatior*, in *Dominici Baudii Amores* (Leyden, 1638). Scriverius prints Saumaise's work on the *P.V.*

STATIUS A., Marginal notes preserved in a transcript of the *editio princeps* as part of *cod*. B 106 of the Bibl. Vallicelliana ; cf. E. CHATELAIN, 'Conjectures d'Achilles Statius sur le *Pervigilium Veneris*', *RPh* IX (1885), 124-6.

TROTSKI J., 'Zum *Pervigilium Veneris*', *Philologus* LXXXI (1926), 339-63.

USSANI V., *In Pervigilium Veneris coniecturae* (Mutina, 1894).

WERNSDORF J. C., *Poetae Latini Minores* VI vols. (Altenburgh, 1780-88, Helmstadt, 1791-99). Cf. vol. III 423-88 for *Pervigilium Veneris*.

WILHELM J. J., *The Cruelest Month* (Yale, 1965).

CONTENTS

2m.25/15.3